A DATE WITH GOD

A Supernatural Visit from the Lord

ALENA KELLEY HARRIS

WESTBOW
PRESS®
A DIVISION OF THOMAS NELSON
& ZONDERVAN

WestBow Press books may be ordered through booksellers or by contacting:

WestBow Press
A Division of Thomas Nelson & Zondervan
1663 Liberty Drive
Bloomington, IN 47403
www.westbowpress.com
1 (866) 928-1240

ISBN: 978-1-9736-1926-0 (sc)
ISBN: 978-1-9736-1925-3 (hc)
ISBN: 978-1-9736-1927-7 (e)

Library of Congress Control Number: 2018901610

Print information available on the last page.

WestBow Press rev. date: 05/14/2018

This book is dedicated to my husband Tony Harris. Thank you for loving me unconditionally as Christ loved the church. God has used you in an amazing way to grant me my happily ever after. I love you Baby love!

CONTENTS

FOREWORD

A Date with God: The book written and
authored by Alena Kelley Harris

In this writing, Alena Kelley
Harris expresses when her
focus and perspective changed.
God revealed His purpose and
plan for her life. Each chapter
gives an in-depth description
on how God pursued Alena.
There are many foundational
truths from the introduction to
the conclusion in this writing.
Jeremiah 29:13 *"And ye shall
seek me and find me when ye shall
search for me with all your heart."*
Holman Christian Standard
Bible. *A Date with God*; a must
read for all thirsty souls, who
are on a conquest for God's best.

Truly for His Service,
Prophet Zebelum K. Rushing

ACKNOWLEDGEMENTS

I would like to acknowledge my Lord and Savior Jesus Christ. The one and only true Living God who commissioned me to write this book and gave me the beautiful title *"A Date with God"*. Without God, I am nothing.

Next, my husband, I appreciate you for looking over the book a thousand times. You made several corrections and encouraged me to finish the book. Then, I would like to thank my spiritual parents, Moma Delisha and Prophet Rushing for encouraging me, praying for me, and speaking life into this book.

To my Aunt Connie Adams, and my good friends Chasity E. Gilland and Star Mckinney thank you so much for your contributions. I appreciate the sacrifices each one of you made so unselfishly.

There is an extra special thank you in my heart for my loving mother, Sonia. She has been on this journey with me from the conception, to the birth, and delivery of this book.

There definitely wouldn't be a book without God and her. I wrote my thoughts and my story, but she has been the mastermind behind the editing, corrections, and making the book flow perfectly. Mom,

I truly appreciate all of the hard work, countless hours, long nights, and years of editing that you have put into this book.

I am forever grateful to God; and truly appreciative to my wonderful family and friends that have contributed to this book in any way. I honor you Father God and give you all the glory!

Thank you Mom.

INTRODUCTION

All of my life, I lived a fairy tale dream, wanting to be like Cinderella, or a princess out of a storybook. I dreamed a prince would someday come and rescue me and sweep me off my feet, and we would live happily ever after. This fairy tale dream has burned in my heart like a continuous flame since I was a little girl.

But this book is not about fairy tales. It is about being a woman who learned that God loves her so much, and all along He knew about the flame that burned inside her heart. As a matter of fact, He is the one who put it there.

From the time we are old enough to imagine what love is, we have all desired to be loved. The Lord revealed to me that the desire to be loved actually came from Him, because God *is* love, and He loves all of His children so much.

> *"Anyone who does not love does not know God,*
> *because God is love" (1 John 4:8 ESV).*

When the Lord opened my understanding to the compassionate and eternal love He has always had for me, I committed my heart to loving Him in return. It was at that moment I began to realize that the Lord, the infinite Creator of all ages, had custom designed a perfect plan for my life!

Like an artist stroking His brush on a canvas or an architect skillfully designing a skyscraper, or a welder giving all his mind and strength to create a work of iron, the Lord, the Maker of heaven and earth had already drawn up a perfect and beautiful blueprint for my life.

> "For I know the plans I have for you," declares the Lord,
> "plans to prosper you and not to harm you, plans to give
> you hope and a future" (Jeremiah 29:11 NIV).

Unfortunatcly, it was not until my heart had been broken over and over again by failed relationships, broken promises, and trying to love someone who did not love me, that God revealed to me that we will never know what true love really is until we have had *A Date with God.*

So, fasten your seat belt! There is no more waiting and wondering if your knight in shining armor will ever come. For the King of Kings and Lord of Lords has arrived to take your heart to a place it has never been before, and it is a place filled and overflowing with nothing but *love!*

1

THE FORGOTTEN ONE

The first truth God wants you to know is that He loves you. The second is He has not forgotten about you. Sometimes it seems as if He has, especially when you have been waiting for what seems like an eternity, and your soul mate still has not come. I want to encourage you to be patient as I help you understand the process of allowing the Lord to align your life with the destiny He has for you.

It's only natural for our heart to long for and desperately desire to be loved by the man or woman of our dreams. The good news is that the Lord knows who He has designed for you, but the relationship can only be established according to His will, not ours!

God, in his infinite wisdom, has a perfect time for everything. Oftentimes, He waits to make sure we are prepared for the blessing before He releases it. In some cases, if God blessed you right now with the perfect mate and you had not committed yourself to a loving relationship with Him first, then, sadly you could end up loving the person more than you love God. The Bible describes this as idolatry, which means having an extreme amount of love and admiration for someone or something. To do so, breaks God's first commandment.

"Thou shall have no other gods before me" (Exodus 20:3 KJV).

Isn't it strange how we devote most of our lives to everything and everyone except the Lord who loves us so much? He has to fight for our time and attention, and we rarely give Him anything in return. We rarely pick up our Bibles or even a book that teaches us of His love for us. Yet He longs for more than our time; He longs for our hearts. God longs to have a loving relationship with us.

The Bible tells us God *is* love! So, let us listen to how He describes Himself: "Love is patient and kind. Love is not jealous, boastful, proud or rude. Love does not demand its own way. Love is not irritable, and love keeps no record of being wrong. Love does not rejoice about injustice but rejoices whenever the truth wins out. Love never gives up, never loses faith, is always hopeful, and endures through every circumstance" (1 Corinthians 13:4–7 NLT).[1]

So, take the time and ponder over what true love is, and then ask yourself if this is the kind of love you want.

We are a work in progress, and while none of us possess all the attributes of God, as His children we must never stop striving daily to become like Him.

The book of Genesis tells us that we are created in the image of God, and He has designed the details of our eyes, hair, and shapes—and even the color of our skin. You are so special that the King of Kings has called for you, and He knows your name! He even knows the numbers of hairs you have on your head, and He has extended His hand for a date with you.

> *"Indeed, the very hairs of your head are all numbered. Don't be afraid; you are worth more than many sparrows" (Luke 12:7 NIV).*

The very essence of who we are is in Him. He knows everything about us, but the question is, do we know Him? So how can the Lord who created us and knows all about us be in relationship with someone who knows nothing about Him?

It's impossible! Because you can't be in a relationship with someone you don't know. We may say we are in a relationship, but it takes time to build relationships even in the natural world. To create

---
[1]

a relationship, you have to spend time with the person to learn things about him or her, such as his or her likes and dislikes. And when you love someone, you even adapt your lifestyle to please this person.

We also have expectations when it comes to relationships. We expect to be loved and to be shown compassion, respect, intimacy, and consideration. We even long for someone who will be faithful to us because no one wants to be cheated on.

So, what about our relationship with God? How much time are we spending to build our relationships with Him? Are we concerned about His likes and dislikes—about the things that please Him and the things that break His heart?

We chase after the things of the world—a relationship with a man or woman, money, houses, cars, clothes, or fame. We consistently chose many of these things over Him, and after we receive them, we're still not satisfied.

Did you ever stop and think that God has feelings too and that we break His heart when we place all these things before Him?

Then, when someone breaks our hearts and our hopes are unfulfilled, we cry out to Him in prayer. We run back to Him, wounded, yet rarely do we consider how we have treated Him. Yet, He loves us all over again. God has always been faithful in His love for us, but are we faithful in our love for Him?

As creatures of free will, we will never be forced by God to enter into a relationship with Him. God wants to be our first love, but when He is not, the wait for our soul mates could be prolonged until He becomes first. He wants to be number one in our lives, but when He is not, He allows us to make our own decisions and choices in relationships.

Unfortunately, we often make choices according to our desires rather than according to the will God has for us. By doing so, we often forfeit the true love, joy, and peace God originally intended for our lives. However, it's not until we can comprehend the love He has for us that we will be able to put all the other relationships in their proper perspective.

God is the source of love, and the Bible tells us, "Every good and perfect gift is from above, coming down from the Father of the heavenly lights, who does not change like shifting shadows" (James 1:17 NIV). He is the Creator of all living things, and He has so beautifully written a script for each one of our lives.

We are the crown and glory of His creation, and He simply adores us. He knows every thought and flight of imagination we have ever had, and He has promised to give us the desires of our hearts, as long as our desires are aligned with His will.

The issues of life and bad relationships can leave us broken, but God wants to put our broken hearts back together. He is the lover of our souls, and He alone holds the key to our happily ever after.

So do not worry, beloved. God has not forgotten about you. If you will allow Him, He only wants to shape and mold you, into the person He originally purposed for you to be. When we allow Him to do so, His perfect plans will begin to unfold in our lives.

"Then the word of the Lord came to me. He said, can I not do with you, Israel, as this potter does? Declares the Lord. Like clay in the hand of the potter, so are you in my hand, Israel" (Jeremiah 18:5–6 NIV).

A DATE WITH GOD

~~~God is head over heels in love with you.~~~

So how could the Lord our God forget about us when He is head over heels in love with us?

That's impossible! While others may criticize us, God still loves us—and it does not matter about our size, our color, or the texture of our hair! We are fearfully and wonderfully made in His sight, and when God looks at us, all He sees is how beautiful we are to Him.

Everything God has created is good. We are the King's sons and daughters! The apple of His eye! The hopes of His dreams and the fulfillments of His purpose! God has great plans in store for us, if only we will allow Him to lead us into our destinies.

Believe it or not, God alone holds the key to your destiny, and He has placed the key inside of you. As you walk more closely with Him and allow His love to embrace you, He will reveal the truth your heart has been longing to hear.

Therefore, I ask for your patience, as this book will take you on my own personal journey. This journey will illustrate how God pursued my love and how I rejected Him over and over again. However, He would not stop until I accepted a "date with Him." What I did not realize was that God was actually setting me up for my happily ever after.

And as you will see, God has not forgotten about you either!

2

THE INVITATION

*S*o, what does an invitation for a date with God look or feel like?

What should you expect, since the Lord does not send an e-vite or use text messages? Neither does He have a personal page on Facebook, Instagram, Snapchat, or Twitter, and I don't think we will find His invitation in the mail, but who knows? He did say nothing is impossible for Him, so I am not ruling anything out.

So, the best way for me to describe the invitation is to share with you how He approached me. An invitation from the Lord is so supernatural, and difficult for me to explain—but I will try.

The inspiration to write this book wasn't just an idea I came up with, but I received the most loving and compassionate invitation from the Lord one day as I was spending time with Him in prayer.

It was around the summer of 2003, and as I had done in the past, I promised to rededicate my life to the Lord and this time I wanted to walk faithfully with Him. I had committed myself to fasting and praying, and during that time, I would spend quality time in my prayer closet worshipping the Lord, reading my bible and playing my praise and worship music. I would stay in my closet for endless hours worshipping Him until I would fall asleep.

As I lay in His presence, the Holy Spirit spoke to me in the most loving and peaceful voice and asked me, "Alena will you go on a date with me?" I told the Lord yes. He instructed me to run bath water and light candles and place them on my bathtub and play my worship music, which He knows I love. I humbly obeyed the voice of God and followed every one of His instructions. When I am in His presence, His power fills the room as He begins to speak to me.

As I basked in His presence, the Lord spoke to me and told me He wanted me to write this book titled, "A Date with God." He told me He wanted to use this book to help others discover how much He loves His people. I responded to the Lord and told Him yes, I would write the book, and this is how one of my most important dates with God began.

It was such a close and intimate time just loving the Lord. On this date, He told me how much He loved me, and how He has taken great detail in creating me. He said He wanted to teach me what real beauty is, inside and out. He showed me the power of His anointing and how it would attract the right person into my life, as well as repel the wrong person.

Have you ever found yourself at a place in your life where it seems everything is going wrong, or maybe everything is going right, but for some strange reason you still feel like something is missing? Most of the time we aren't sure what the problem is, yet we know it's something significant. Many times, we try to ignore it, or we wear a mask as if everything is okay. But deep down inside we know something is not right.

It took me a while to realize what I was experiencing was actually an invitation from God, and His love was pursuing me. He was tugging at my heart when life felt empty; friends had forsaken me, and when nothing seemed to satisfy.

To be honest, most of the time when God extended His invitation to me, I couldn't describe what was going on in my life, but for some reason, I would feel His loving presence when I was going through the most chaotic times. Usually, it was when I was in a place God never intended for me to be. However, His timing is always perfect because He knows when our heart is open, and our ears are eager to hear a Word from the Lord. He loves us, and He knows when we have reached the end of our rope. Usually, it's during those times we will be willing to listen.

I believe all of us, at some point in our lives, have experienced emptiness and had no clue why we were feeling that way. During those times, I thought I needed a man, but later I realized God is the only one who can fill the void in our lives. He is the only one who knows how our hearts have been broken, will not talk about us, or share our deepest secrets. He is the only one who understands us and in spite of our faults and mistakes, He is the only one we can trust, to love us unconditionally. It was during those seasons of emptiness I was experiencing an invitation from God.

Countless times I have run from His invitation not realizing He is the only one who can give me what I need the most—the love and peace of God. This is what an invitation from God felt like to me.

So, an invitation from the Lord is His loving way of trying to draw us to a place where we can rest in Him and cast all of our cares on Him because He cares for us. God is the lover of our soul, and He longs to be a part of our lives. He wants to love us and lavish us with everything we need, and our heart could ever desire.

Jesus said, "Come to me, all you who are weary and burdened, and I will give you rest" (Matthew 11:28 NIV). As we experience these overwhelming emotions an invitation of love is reaching out to us because God wants to have a deeper relationship. It is the one relationship most of us have been missing all of our lives. It is an invitation to spend time with the Lord and hear His voice in a new and special way and to trust Him without limitations. It is an invitation to release all of our hurts, fears, guilt, shame, and rejection and finally be loved and learn how to love like never before.

How do we allow God to love us, and how do we love Him in return? To be able to love Him in return, you must be centered in His love. This means we daily position ourselves to spend time in prayer, reading and meditating on His word. Then, after we learn the truth, we make it our goal to daily do those things that please Him. By doing these things, we build our relationship with God and experience the love of God, which leads us to the peace of God.

Am I saying I am walking in perfection? No! As you will learn from my journey, we must learn to walk daily with a conscious awareness that God loves us. He also wants to be loved by us because He alone knows the plans He has for our lives.

During our daily walk with Him, we may make mistakes, but we learn from them and don't allow them to become crutches; instead, we use them as stepping-stones that bring us closer to our destiny and back into right alignment with our Creator.

You see, every time I strayed away from my relationship with the Lord, I was no longer able to enjoy the peace of God. Undoubtedly, it took place in my life when I was on a crash course to do what Alena wanted to do, rather than what God wanted Alena to do.

It is during those times I begin to feel depleted, but it's also during those times the Lord always shows up with an invitation in the most loving way. He knocks at the door of my heart, asking me to come and spend more time with Him, because when I am in His presence, this is when I experience the peace of God.

The Bible tells us love, joy, and peace are all fruits of the Holy Spirit. Your money can't buy them neither will your occupation nor your title, no matter how high your earthly position is.

You may drive a Bentley, live in a mansion, dress in the most expensive clothes, or have the finest shape in town, but as long as your relationship is disconnected from God, you will not be able to enjoy the fruits of His Spirit. These belong to God because they are exclusively His and can never be found in material things.

> *"But the fruit of the Spirit is love, joy, peace, forbearance, kindness, goodness, faithfulness, gentleness and self-control" (Galatians 5:22, 23 NIV).*

We may experience temporary fun or excitement, but the Bible tells us the pleasures of sin are only for a season, and seasons don't last very long. Therefore, during the times when my relationship was disconnected from God, no matter where I searched, I could not find peace, only emptiness because I was outside of the Will of God.

I encourage you to allow the invitation from the Lord to be your navigation system because His GPS (God's Personal Spirit) has always been there to help us, especially when He detects we have lost our way. When I am lost, I need the Holy Spirit to point me in the right direction. I believe when we follow His instructions, He will lead us along the pathway of peace because His love is always saying,

> *"I am the way and the truth and the life" (John14: 6 KJV).*

Did you know God chose you before the foundation of the world just to love you? That is why He is extending an invitation to you and invitations are not randomly sent to anyone, but only to those chosen by God. John 15:16 the word declares, "You did not choose me, but I chose you." If you are reading this book, you can rest assured God chose you and that makes you His VIP.

This is an invitation of love and all He desires from us is to be loved in return with all of our heart, mind, and soul. Someone He can call His very own. Sound familiar?

I am sure it does, because this is what we desire in a relationship: someone we can call our husband or wife. Well, God feels the same way about you and me, but it took me a long time to realize this. His word declares,

> "I am your husband" (Jeremiah 3:14 NIV)

> "You did not choose me, but I chose you and appointed you so that you might go and bear fruit—fruit that will last—and so that whatever you ask in My Name the Father will give you" (John 15:16)

Do you realize being chosen by God is the highest calling you will ever have on your life? To be selected for a position of authority can't compare to being chosen by God.

Therefore, when He knocks at the doors of our heart and beckons for our love, time and devotion, He finds us alone and searching for love in all the wrong places. Instead of searching for Him, we go from one relationship to another looking for someone who will love us and fill the emptiness in our heart that only He can fill.

He extends an invitation of love to us, because we are chosen, but so often we refuse to accept Him. Yet, through His loving kindness and tender mercies, He continues to draw us to Him because He wants to provide for us and protect us. He proves His love for us by opening doors we thought were impossible to go through.

He blesses us with jobs and promotions, yet we don't realize His Word declares that promotion does not come from the north or the south; it comes from the Lord. The wisdom and knowledge we possess are gifts from God.

But instead of giving Him our love in return, or even showing Him how much we appreciate all He has done for us, many times we do not give Him the time of day. As a matter of fact, we do everything in our power to give our love to someone who really does not deserve it.

If only our hearts and minds could comprehend the love God has for us, we would realize that this is where true love begins and there is no greater love or invitation!

"But you are a chosen people, a royal priesthood, a holy nation, God's special possession, that you may declare the praises of Him who called you out of darkness into His wonderful light" (1 Peter 2:9 NIV).

In my personal experience, I endured so much heartache before I realized, I was chosen by God and loving Him should have always been my first priority. He is the first knight in shining armor that has tried over and over again to rescue His princess and prove His love to her because He wants to be our first love. Not second, not after everyone else has deserted us; neither does He want to be our part-time lover. God wants to be first! Therefore, we cannot put another "god"—which means people, places, or things—before Him.

"For the Lord your God, who is among you, is a jealous God" (Deuteronomy 6:15 NIV).

~~~~~~~~~~~~~~~~~

Now listen, beloved, there is a ringing at the door of your heart! A ringing in your ears! It is a sound from the heavenly host and at long last, your invitation has arrived, and to your surprise, it is the King of Glory.

But, as the King enters with His invitation, He finds His beloved at a time when her heart is broken. A loss of appetite and her spirit is low because what she once thought was true love filled her life only temporarily, and now it is gone, and she is all alone. Her world has stopped because the one she trusted, the one she loved, the one she gave up everything for, has abandoned her. The question tearing her heart apart is, why?

These are her thoughts, her hurts, her feelings, her cries, but what she does not realize is that God's invitation is eternal, and His love for her will never end. Even though she was giving her love to another, He will not leave her; neither will He forsake her. He watches as she cries and catches every tear that falls from her eyes. When she thought He was not listening to her prayers, He has been there all the time!

"You keep track of all my sorrows. You have collected all my tears in your bottle. You have recorded each one in your book" (Psalm 56:8 NIV).

I encourage you to open your heart because God wants to wrap you in the comfort of His loving arms, heal every hurt, and every disappointment you have ever had. If only you will allow the Lord our God to take you into His secret chamber, His throne room, and reveal to you the beauty of His love.

A DATE WITH GOD

~~~*There is no greater love.*~~~

Oh, how I wish I could turn back the hands of time and give the Lord all the love I tried to give to someone who didn't appreciate it. To be honest, those I tried to love did not know how to love me.

I can recall being a socialite trying to make all the major events and parties hoping to find love. It was so ridiculous because the husband God had for me was never at any of those events. He had lost his desire to do any of those things, because he also had received an invitation from God. It was after he accepted his invitation from the Lord and began walking in obedience to the Word of God, that God begin preparing him to connect with me.

The reality is that any man or woman who does not have a relationship with the Lord is also broken. Therefore, how can you expect a person who is broken and possibly struggling with issues from their past, be able to heal your hurts and give you the love you need? When he or she is in need of an invitation from God themselves. That is something you cannot give to another person, it is between that person and God and just like God is waiting for you, He is also waiting for that person too!

So, don't give up. As long as the King is on the throne, all hope is not gone.

> *"Love the Lord your God with all your heart and with all your soul and with all your mind. This is the first and greatest commandment. And the second is like it: Love your neighbor as yourself" (Matthew 22:37–39 NIV).*

~~~*Do not rush your relationship.*~~~

We all want to have our happily ever after, but we cannot rush God and believe me, I tried. After I accepted my invitation from the Lord, I watched Him answer prayers and petitions I had placed before Him twenty-two years earlier. The Lord fulfilled prophecies and promises spoken into my life regarding my husband, which I thought would never come to pass.

It is God's will to give us the desires of our heart, but it will only happen according to His timing. Therefore, we must be patient and wait on the Lord and be of good courage. God has to prepare us for our soul mates, as well as prepare our soul mates for us.

We are instructed to not be anxious for anything; however, there were times when I became impatient, and I was tempted to make things happen by forcing a relationship before God's timing.

The Lord told me I could mess things up with my future husband by chasing him. Therefore, I had to be patient because my husband was watching me, and he wanted someone to love him for himself. My husband knew I was attracted to him, and he was to me. The Lord told me he was trapped in a sour relationship, but it was not going to last.

The Lord also told me, when He brought him out, he would need me as a friend spiritually and not as a lover. I was told not to worry about being in the right place at the right time because God is in control and, just as He allowed us to meet the first time, God would control the situation again.

The Lord instructed me to treat my relationship with my future husband as if I was carrying a baby because receiving the promises of God is like being pregnant. When you're pregnant you watch what you eat and try to do everything correct. We do this because we are about to give birth to the promises God has spoken over our lives. Naturally, the sperm and egg connect, then it takes nine months to nurture and care for the promise.

God wanted me close to Him so I could hear His voice. He instructed me, if I entered the relationship prematurely, before His timing and became sexually involved, the relationship would not be built on my love and obedience to God; instead, it would be formed according to my own sensual desires. This would cause me to end up in God's permissive will and not His perfect will.

The late prophet, Aida Porter prophesied, "God is instructing you to be patient and to wait for Him to bring His promises to pass because He does not need your help." Immediately after Prophet Aida spoke those words, the Lord spoke to me and said He would confirm the prophecy she had spoken from written His Word:

> "Promise me, O women of Jerusalem, not to awaken love
> until the time is right" (Songs of Solomon 8:4 NLT).

Once Christ awakens us to His love and reveals the plans He has for our lives, we must become committed to building a close relationship with Him. Being close to Him is how we learn His will for our lives. We must make a special effort to learn more about Him. This will cause our faith to grow, so we can become strong and committed in our walk with Him.

We must pray and use the Word of God to remind ourselves of the plans He has for us. Then, we must be patient and wait for His promises to come to pass, if not, we could fall back into bad habits and relationships, which rob us of our blessings. The truth of God's love has come to open our eyes and to reveal to us the path that leads to our destiny.

We have to realize God is timeless and eternal. We may feel we have wasted so much time and made countless mistakes, but when we ask for forgiveness and mean it with all of our hearts, God can redeem the time we have lost. If we remain faithful in our walk with the Lord, He is still able to turn our situations around.

"And I will restore to you the years… (Joel 2:25)

"And we know all things work together for good to them that love God, to them who are the called according to His purpose" (Romans 8:28 KJV).

The King has an invitation just for you, and I encourage you to say yes and begin seeking Him while He can still be found. Open the door to your heart and allow the King of Glory to come into your life where He will do the most amazing and phenomenal things you could ever imagine.

The Lord is inviting us to move beyond ourselves and into a covenant relationship and become connected forever with the lover of our soul. So, do not rush the relationship, because the love He has to offer you will last for a lifetime!

3

THE FIRST DATE

*J*f you have reached this chapter, my prayer is that your heart is longing for more and you have embraced the opportunity for a date with God. But since this date is like no other, don't be surprised if your friends do not understand why you no longer have an interest in going to the places you use to go or doing the things you use to do. But that is okay! Because a date with God is an individual invitation just for you! It does not mean your friends will not receive their invitations one day. But today, the date has been arranged for *you!* And the mystery of a date with God is that He is the only one who can set it up.

So how is a date with God arranged? Because He is God, there are countless ways He can approach you, but often He will speak directly to your spirit. He may have a friend or even a stranger approach you to confirm God wants you to get closer to Him. Nevertheless, deep in your heart, you will know God is trying to get your attention. He may use a blessing or even a tragic situation to let you know He is pursuing you. You can't plan it, fake it, or pretend, because God is all seeing and all knowing, therefore, you cannot come to Him except He invites you!

> *"No one can come to me unless the Father who*
> *sent me draws them" (John 6:44 NIV).*

You see, the Holy One of Israel—the Great I am—is requesting a date with you. Therefore, you should never allow anyone or anything to become a priority before the King.

Now, let us take a look at some very exceptional women who were chosen to experience some unforgettable dates with God.

Mary—The Mother of Jesus

Mary, the mother of Jesus, received a royal invitation. It was hand delivered by the angel Gabriel in a town in Galilee. Mary was a virgin pledged to marry a man name Joseph, a descendant of David.

When the angel appeared to Mary, he said, "Greetings, you are highly favored! The Lord is with you" (Luke 1:28 NIV). "I am the Lord's servant, Mary answered. May your word to me be fulfilled" (Luke 1:38 NIV). If you listen closely to Mary's response, you will hear her submission to the Lord, her willingness to serve and her faith.

Although I was not there, I can only imagine what it felt like as the Holy Spirit overshadowed Mary, wrapping all of His love around her. As His Spirit saturated her body, soul, and mind with the pure power of His love, Mary experienced a powerful encounter with the Almighty God.

This visitation was not sensual; instead, it was a holy and sacred encounter with God, and Mary believed everything He had promised: The Son of God would be conceived through a humble girl who trusted in Him. Can you imagine what it must have felt like to experience such a mind-blowing encounter?

Mary knew people would talk about her because it appeared she had become pregnant out of wedlock. I am sure she was greatly troubled, but she did not let trouble stop her! I am sure she was afraid, but she did not let fear stop her! I am sure people thought she was crazy when they heard the Holy Spirit had impregnated her, but she did not let what people thought about her, or said about her, stop her. Mary's encounter was so supernatural.

When we look at creation, we can see that God's ways are not our ways because how can we explain the process that takes place after the seed of a man connects with the egg in a woman's womb to create a child? Miraculously, a skeletal frame begins to form and every organ necessary for the body to function. Then, nine months later, a child is born! Just in childbearing alone, we see His miraculous power. Glory to God!

Life itself is one of the most phenomenal miracles we will ever experience. So, if you have been asking God for a miracle, I encourage you to take a look in the mirror! Because you are a miracle! Therefore, when you receive the revelation that God is calling you, do not let anything stop you from answering His call!

An encounter with God blessed Mary beyond her wildest imagination. Now just imagine this same God is requesting a date with you.

Esther—A woman of great faith

Next, let's take a look at Esther, a Jewish woman of great faith who God used to stop a conspiracy to kill the nation of Jews; God's chosen people. Esther was raised in an average home by her uncle, Mordecai, but had no idea she would be transformed from an average young woman to one day becoming a queen.

God positioned this anointed woman to become wife to the king who had the power to stop the execution. I will speak more about the courageous act of Esther in the final chapter.

Ruth—Loyal to Naomi, and faithful to her God

Next, we will look at Ruth, whose husband died, yet she refused to disconnect from her mother-in-law, Naomi. This ordained connection led Ruth to meet her husband, Boaz.

Naomi has been described as the female Job of the Bible, illustrating a woman's perspective of suffering and loss, yet God restored everything back to her through her daughter-in-law Ruth.

Ruth and Boaz gave birth to a son who became the father of Jesse. Jesse was the father of King David, which made Ruth his great grandmother. The words spoken by Ruth are symbolic of our relationship with Christ and the marriage vows many use today during wedding ceremonies:

> "Don't urge me to leave you or to turn back from you. Where you go I will go, and where you stay I will stay. Your people will be my people and your God my God" (Ruth 1:16 NIV).

Sarah—A mother of nations

Then there is Sarah, the wife of Abraham. Sarah was ninety-nine years old when God told Abraham that Sarah would become pregnant with a son. Sarah laughed, but God said, "Is anything too hard for the Lord?" (Genesis 18:14, KJV). When God makes a promise, He cannot lie!

The Bible tells us Sarah's womb was as good as dead, but in spite of her age, she received a date with God and gave birth to a son, Isaac, just as God had promised. The Lord prophesied to this woman, well stricken in age and told Abraham, "I will bless her and will surely give you a son by her. I will bless her so that she will be the mother of nations; kings of peoples will come from her" (Genesis 17:16, NIV). Glory to God!

What if Sarah had given up and aborted her dream and her baby; she would have missed her greatest blessing. As I stated earlier, waiting for God is similar to birthing a child; therefore, you must carry the promise to full term to receive the blessing. When we connect with God, His will begins to form in our hearts and minds. Then, at the appointed time, we will experience the manifestation of all He has in store for us.

In many ways, these women were just like you and me. They were hurt, rejected, frightened, and doubtful, but they were all women of great faith who dared to believe, and they all experienced miraculous dates with God. There were also great men of the bible who experienced a date with God. Abraham had to leave all of his family to experience his date with God. Moses gave up the riches of this world and chose to follow God to save his people. Jacob's date with God included him wrestling with God until he blessed him.

> "It was by faith that Moses, when he grew up, refused to be called the son of Pharaoh's daughter. He chose to share the oppression of God's people instead of enjoying the fleeting pleasures of sin. He thought it was better to suffer for the sake of Christ than to own the treasures of Egypt, for he was looking ahead to his great reward. It was by faith that Moses left the land of Egypt, not fearing the king's anger. He kept right on going because he kept his eyes on the one who is invisible" (Hebrew 11:24-27, NLT)

A date with God is where it all begins—when God gives you a wakeup call in your spirit, and you begin to sense the longing need and desire to be in His presence. He may or may not tell you exactly what time He is coming, but rest assured, He will keep His promise. Now, it is up to you to invite Him into your heart and then listen for the soft whisper of His voice in your ear. He is coming to see about you, and His timing is always perfect! All you need to do is relax and trust Him.

In our hearts, whether we realized it or not, God has been longing for us to spend time with Him. When we feel lonely, when our hearts are heavy, when we have been hurt or broken, feeling betrayed and rejected, God will tug at our hearts to come to Him and tell Him what is on our minds. These are the times when God beckons us to go on a date with Him.

By now, you may be asking yourself what it would be like to have a date with God. You may feel a little hesitant because you are not sure what a date with God will require of you. In your heart, you believe you are ready to accept His invitation, not knowing what to expect, but longing for more in your life than what you have right now.

If this describes you, you are in a perfect place to experience your first date with God and allow Him to take you to a place you have never been before, experiencing a love you will never experience again in a lifetime.

And I must admit that I have no clue as to what your date will be like, or how or when the Prince of Peace will grace you with His presence. But what I can promise is, if you will begin to hunger and thirst for a relationship with the Lord, to be in His presence and walk in the perfect will He has for your life, He will come and give you living waters and you will never thirst again!

"Blessed are those who hunger and thirst for righteousness,
for they shall be filled" (Matthew 5:6 KJV).

A DATE WITH GOD

~~~*Intimacy is everything.*~~~

As a personal testimony, I have had many miraculous and angelic encounters with God. He is such a gentleman! He will not force us to accept Him, nor force Himself into your daily schedule, but He will patiently wait and allow you to set the mood because intimacy is everything—or should I say worship is everything.

A relationship with the Lord is all about being close and intimate with Him, and this is how we worship Him. As we begin praying and talking to Him, pouring out our love for Him, He will in return pour out His love for us. That's worship! He will speak with you and even give you instructions and wisdom about dealing with the simplest matters of your life because He is genuinely concerned about you.

Intimacy with God is also spending time reading the Bible because this is where you learn about Him, the love He has for us, as well as instructions on how He has planned for us to live our lives on earth.

~~~*Find a secret place where you can meet with God.*~~~

My favorite place to meet with the Lord is in my prayer closet. That is our secret place! I like to listen to CeCe Winans' CD titled, *Throne Room*. The anointing of God on CeCe's voice always ushers in the presence of God. You can also meet Him when you are alone in your car or walking in a park. Just find a place—a secret place to go and be alone and talk to the Lord. Just remember, it doesn't matter where you meet because it's between you and God.

After you have established a place, it is important to set the mood. When you are expecting the love of your life, you prepare for his coming. We want our homes to be presentable and clean when we know he is coming to spend time with us. I personally believe God wants us to bring Him our best, and that is our whole heart.

Remember, this is a relationship. As we do in any relationship, we desire to look beautiful. So, it is okay to adorn yourself as you prepare to meet with the King! There may be times when we do not feel or look our best, but that is okay too. Again, God loves you just the way you are, and your alone time with God will be a blessing beyond your imagination.

One of my greatest fulfillments comes when I praise and worship God in dance. As a praise dancer, I love to wear white because it represents purity and holiness. I recall receiving a prophecy that when I danced the angels were there dancing with me. The prophet also said the Lord showed me dancing with a white scarf in my hand waving it unto the Lord. I knew this prophecy was true because I would do this in my alone time as I danced before the Lord and no one else knew it. Now, just imagine yourself as a queen and allow yourself to feel His love and open your heart to believe, hope, and to love again.

~~~~~~~~~~~~~~~~~~~~~~

This brings me to another revelation I received from the Lord: have you ever dated someone who, when he or she sees the true love and commitment you have for him or her, they tell you, "You are too good for me"?

Well, guess what? Those people are right! However, it is not the *good* they see in you; it is the *God* they see in you. When their lives and lifestyles are not in agreement with God's will for your life, they will not be able to stay.

When we experience relationships in which we have been mistreated, or the person has left us, remember there is a blessing in saying good-bye. Ending a relationship can be very painful. However, holding on to relationships that are ungodly are far more harmful to our well-being than just releasing them and waiting on God. We must realize good-bye is not always a bad thing because God has a way of removing people when we are not strong enough to remove them ourselves. Therefore, God will cause them to walk away and He does this to protect us and to ensure the great plans and destiny He has for our life.

When we spend time in the presence of God, His anointing will attract the person God Has purposed and ordained for our lives. Don't expect him or her to be perfect; after all, we are not. However, he or she will have a true love and respect for God, His ways, and you. We must remember we are all a work in progress, and the Lord will perfect those things concerning us, but we must walk by faith, knowing God has our best interest at heart.

I have been blessed to have many dates with God where He visits me in a dream, speak to me during worship or even in the midst of adversities. Each time my heart is filled with love and gratitude towards Him.

Then, there are times when He finds me broken and at my lowest. I recall one occasion when He told me to get dressed and to fix myself up. Sometimes when our spirits are low, we don't feel good about ourselves and we don't see ourselves the way God sees us. During those times, He doesn't judge us, but encourages us because He loves us and wants us to know He has great things in store for us. God sees us as royalty, and He wants us to always remember who we are to Him.

Many of you have been on dates with God and didn't even know it. A date with God is simply spending alone time with your Savior and sharing your most intimate feelings, thoughts, prayers, desires, worship, and all that is dear to you. God will lead you into the most loving and fulfilling relationship, but you must be willing to let Him love you by committing yourself to a date with God.

We live in a world dominated by social media and the Internet, which makes it easy to become busy and distracted leaving little time—to no time at all—to accept a date with God. Therefore, we must make an individual effort to set priorities and not allow anything to rob us of the time we need to spend in His presence.

Life will always have distractions, but God has given us the power of choice. Therefore, we must choose a designated time with the Lord and make Him our first priority. So, bring your journal, Kleenex, music, and whatever He places on your heart, because I promise you, the time you spend with God will be the most fulfilling time of your life.

~~~*God is a God of order.*~~~

God is a God of order and loving Him always comes first. Next is loving others as we would love ourselves. By doing so, we fulfill every law of God simply by love. Why should we love God more? Because, "In Him, we live, move, and exist" (Acts 17:8 NASB). It is His breath that flows in and out of our lungs each day.

Without God, none of us would exist. He is the source of all life; therefore, we should never exalt another human being above God not even your husband, wife, mother, father or children!

A DATE WITH GOD

"Anyone who loves their father or mother more than me is not worthy of me; anyone who loves their son or daughter more than me is not worthy of me" (Matthew 10:37 NIV).

The love God has for us is so matchless there is no one on earth who will ever love you the way God loves you! His love will surpass the love of any man or woman you will ever meet because He does not just love in words alone; rather, His actions proved how much He loves us.

You see, God is not like some guy or girl who walks up to you and says, "I love you" but makes no sacrifices to prove their love. Jesus sacrificed His life for those who had no affections toward Him, yet, He took the punishment we deserve because He loves us. When God allowed His only begotten Son to sacrifice His life for our sins, He proved His love. That is why He deserves to be our first love.

"But God demonstrates His own love for us in this: While we were still sinners, Christ died for us" (Romans 5:8 NIV).

The Bible tells us, "For without the shedding of blood, there is no forgiveness" (Hebrews 9:22 NLT). Therefore, God wrapped Himself in human flesh and came to earth in the body of His only Son and gave His own life and shed His own blood as the ultimate sacrifice for our sins.

"For God made Christ, who never sinned, to be the offering for our sin, so that we could be made right with God through Christ" (2 Corinthians 5:21 NLT).

Like a sheep being led to the slaughter, He never opened His mouth. He did not try to defend Himself but took the punishment we deserved. His blood covers all our sins—past, present, and future. Now, this is what I call love!

So, if you are looking for somebody to love you, you can stop searching! There is someone who does love you, and His name is Jesus and there is no greater love!

> For at just the right time, while we were still powerless, the Messiah died for the ungodly. For it is rare for anyone to die for a righteous person, though somebody might be brave enough to die for a good person. But God demonstrates His love for us by the fact that the Messiah died for us while we were still sinners. (Romans 5:6–8 ISV)

Jesus said, in order to be accepted into the beloved family of God, we must be born again. Not from our mother's wombs, but with His spirit. A new life begins and the old mind and life of sin is passed away and behold all things have become new. I don't know about you, but I sure needed a second chance to start living the life God ordained for me!

If you believe you need a fresh start with God, just say this prayer:

> Heavenly Father. I was wrong. Will you forgive me? I believe Jesus died for my sins, and on the third day, You raised Him from grave. You said: if I confess Jesus is now Lord of my life, and I believe this in my heart, I shall be saved. Thank you for loving me and forgiving me. Now, I ask Your Holy Spirit to teach me and give me the strength to live for you in Jesus's name!

If you pray this prayer, I welcome you into the beloved family of God. Now ask the Lord to lead you to a Bible teaching and believing church where you can learn the ways of God and how to grow in Christ and become the mature Christian He died for you to become. His Holy Spirit will teach you and give you the power to love and live out the plans God has for your life.

"Follow God's example, therefore, as dearly loved children and walk in the way of love, just as Christ loved us and gave himself up for us as a fragrant offering and sacrifice to God" (Ephesians 5:1–2 NIV.)

Prayer is what led me to my first date with God. Prayer and repentance always open the door to new beginnings. I remember my first date with God. It was so heartwarming. I sang to Him, praised and worshiped Him, and He spoke to my heart. He heard my cry, and He comforted me. If only we knew the depth of His love and the price He paid for a date with us. This was the most expensive date of my life because He paid for it with His blood. With His blood He ransomed me. He forgave me, and He gave me a second chance to live and love again.

God's love overshadowed me, and I knew I was right where I was supposed to be. He had been waiting for me to say yes to Him, to surrender to His love, His will, His way. I had said yes to everything and everyone else, yet it had profited me nothing. And all He wanted was a chance—a chance to make me happy and love me like no other! Tears well up in my eyes as I think about the love He has for me, and I did not even realize it. He had waited so patiently for me to finally realize how much He loved me.

Our search for love can become very frustrating. The journey for true love sometimes feels hopeless. We complain about being twenty-something, thirty-something, and before we know it, we are forty or fifty and still haven't found *"the one."* But have you ever considered how long God has waited for you? Yes, you—the person who is reading this book. He was waiting for you even before you were conceived in your mother's womb. He waited just to let you know you were made to love.

~~~*Overcoming toxic relationships.*~~~

My former pastor, Bishop T. D. Jakes said years ago, "Change can be so difficult at times, and sometimes it can cost you so much to change that you give up on your dreams for the convenience of not having to go through the threat of failure."

I understood what Bishop Jakes was saying because I had walked in those shoes. I had gone back to toxic relationships over and over because I was desperate to be loved! Desperate to have a man! At one point, I thought time was working against me, and I needed to accept the person who was choosing me even though, in my heart, I knew God had not sent him. These types of relationships are like black holes that rob of us of our joy, identity, and ultimately our lives. They take everything from you and give nothing in return. Therefore, I urge you to let go of every relationship you know is not from God.

So how do you know if a relationship is not from God? Well, I encourage you to go on a date with God and ask Him!

Many times, we open up too quickly to people, and they use our openness against us. This happens because we don't go to God in prayer and ask Him, "Is he or she the one?" He is your Father, and He wants you to come to Him first with any questions you may have. This is what builds the relationship between you and God.

He is ready to heal the wounds, and He will never use anything we have done in the past against us. He will never tell anyone our secrets and you can trust Him because He is faithful. Just listen to what the Lord asks us to do:

A DATE WITH GOD

"Come now, let's settle this,' says the Lord. 'Though your sins are like scarlet, I will make them as white as snow. Though they are red like crimson, I will make them as white as wool" (Isaiah 1:18–19, NLT).

All you need to do is go on a date with God and tell Him everything that is in your heart. God loves you, and He has put your past behind you. You must learn to do the same. He wants to settle this matter of the heart because your future is brighter than you could ever imagine.

I hope by now you are beginning to feel safe in His arms. His love can be felt in every word and every whisper. For the first time in a long time, you can feel safe as you begin to open up. God holds a place in our hearts that only He can fill. When we try to fill this void with other things or people, we are left empty with holes in our hearts.

As we begin to allow Him into our lives and we open up our heart, His love will begin to shine a light on the deception of the enemy. The Lord will begin to expose the lies with the truth, and before you know it, the pain will be replaced with peace and unselfish love.

You may not realize it, but what you are experiencing right now is your date with God and His love for you. True love should be the greatest feeling in the world, and if you have not experienced this, then you have not been on a date with God.

You may want to run and tell someone, and God will let you know who is worthy of knowing, but some things—the secret things of God—are to be just between you and Him. So be careful and don't reveal everything to everybody. Some things we have to ponder in our hearts just as Mary, the mother of Jesus, did. Everyone will not understand your date with God, however, you must guard and protect your relationship.

~~~God has great things in store for me!~~~

Women and men of God, when the time comes for you to be presented to your husband or wife, God's anointing will be all over you. You will stand out, and the attraction will not be based solely on your physical appearance. What your husband or wife will see in you goes beyond what is on the outside.

Men of God, I also encourage you to say yes to a date with God. Not only will it free you, but it will open so many doors to your future, including the wife God has ordained for you. She may be currently trapped in the wrong relationship or in bondage to the enemy, but your love and obedience to God could be the key to setting her free. Your future life and family are waiting for you. You need only to say yes to a date with God and surrender your life to Him. Jesus is the only one capable of setting the captive free, and your yes to Him will free both of you.

The reason the man's date with God is the most important decision in his life is that God ordained him to be the head of the family. Once your life has come into alignment with the Will of God, every door the enemy has shut for all these years will finally began to open. I am excited about your future!

~~~Love God the right way.~~~

Loving God is not going to church every Sunday; the devil knows how to do that. Loving God is a lifestyle, a relationship, and a commitment. To know this kind of love, you have to forgive everyone who has hurt you and let go of the guilt and bitterness of the past.

When you forgive, you are setting two people free, and one of them is you. Forgive fully and deeply within your heart, and quickly forgive. If calling or visiting the person who hurt you or whom you hurt is too much, just give it to God. It is not always necessary to have a conversation to make peace; sometimes it is simply taking it to God and letting go.

*"I have come that they may have life, and have
it to the full" (John 10:10 NIV).*

There is a new beginning on the horizon, a new love in the air, a new life that is just for you and it will cause you to smile on the inside. As the night approaches, we don't want our date to end. God is the lover of our souls, and we are finally starting to understand His love for us. You may be wondering when your next date will be and you pray every night could be as perfect as tonight.

4

THE FIRST TOUCH

God is a Spirit; therefore, there are so many ways He can touch our lives. When He visits me in dreams, I feel as if I have been "touched by an angel," and my heart is filled with so much hope and excitement. His love is all around me, and I don't want the night to end. So just like the perfect date, He promises to show up in my dreams once again, and He does.

In my dreams, I can feel His presence and His love as it illuminates my entire soul. It feels like I'm having an out-of-body experience as I watch Him roll the film of my life and unveil the plans He has for me. I wake up feeling the emotions from the dream because the experience feels incredibly real.

I believe God touches us through dreams and visions; therefore, it is very important to write your dreams down and then seek God for an interpretation. God has given me the gift of interpreting dreams. Each time He gives me a dream, I write it down. Many of the things He has revealed to me have already manifested.

~~~Love letters written to God.~~~

I began writing letters to God several years ago. Each time I poured my heart out to Him for different reasons. In some of my letters I shared my prayers and concerns, but so many times I wrote letters to the Lord just to tell Him how much I loved Him, and how much I appreciated Him loving me and forgiving me over and over again.

Hello Father:

Today has been truly been blessed. I had the opportunity to tell somebody about you and your love. I ask you today to keep my heart clean and keep your Word in my heart that I may not sin against you. Teach me your Word and Your ways, that I may reflect Your ways in me. Continue to show me mercy and love. Help me Lord, I need you and want you in my life. Thank you, Jesus. Glory be unto God. Love Alena – January 5, 2003 1:00 a.m.

"First seek ye the Kingdom of God and His righteousness, and all these things will be added unto you" (Matthew 6:33 KJV).

In another one of my letters, I told the Lord I didn't want to be hurt anymore by another man. I asked the Lord to help me because I felt as if I was in a fight for my life and needed Him more than ever before.

Dear God:

Thank You so much for just loving me and forgiving me time after time. Please lead me and guide me in the right way and teach me how to live a life pleasing to You. This I ask in Jesus's name. Love Alena

This type of letter is really a cry out to God for forgiveness because many times during my walk with God, I became distracted or had gone down the wrong path. I was so tired of being hurt and ashamed and that's why I poured my heart out in a letter to the Lord. I asked Him to please give me the patience to wait for the soul mate He had chosen for me. I knew the Lord was the only one who could help me and heal my broken heart.

I shared earlier that dreams are just one of the ways God can touch us; and writing love letters to God is one of the ways we can touch Him.

Communication is key in any relationship; therefore, we need to continuously talk to the Lord and this is known as prayer. When we pray, this is an opportunity to open up and talk to Him because this is the only way we can establish a loving relationship with Him.

Therefore, I spoke to the Lord in my letters as my loving father and told him I was willing to give love, but I wanted to be loved in return. I trusted His love, and I knew He was willing and able to be everything I needed Him to be. I desired to be strong and faithful in my walk with the Lord and I was counting on Him because, He was the only One I could trust.

Many times, one person in a relationship places all of the responsibility on the other person to fill their emptiness, and it drives that person away. Again, we are asking a person to be something to us that only God can be. Because like us they too have suffered from rejection, hurt, and the pain of abandonment. They desire to receive love, but don't know how to give love. Therefore, it becomes a challenge for them because most of them did not have fathers or mothers to love them growing up. They were never taught how to love; neither have they been shown real love in their own lives.

No one can give what he or she does not have. Then, when things don't work out as expected, we find our lives going in circles, from one painful, disappointing relationship to another. In essence, we are asking another human being to do the impossible.

Only God can heal our broken hearts and fill the void inside. When He sees us this way, this is when He seizes the opportunity to demonstrate again how much He loves us. He may manifest His love through a song, a miracle, an unexpected blessing, in the appearance of a cloud, and even a book as He tries to prove His love for us.

~~~My first miracle of love was an
encounter with an angel.~~~

God is capable of performing so many miracles and speaking to us in so many miraculous ways. One day I was down and out and felt as if I was not loved. I wanted to be close to my heavenly Father because I was hurting, and I needed to hear from Him. I needed a touch from the Lord. I was desperate to be in His presence and felt like the woman with the issue of blood. If I could just touch the hem of His garment, I knew I would be made whole.

"And, behold, a woman, which was diseased with an issue
of blood twelve years, came behind him, and touched the hem
of his garment: For she said within herself, If I may but touch
his garment, I shall be whole" (Matthew 9:21–22 KJV).

I was an emotional wreck, but I gathered my strength and kept crying out to the Lord. As the feeling of being unloved seemed overwhelming, I looked up at the sky and saw a beautiful white cloud in the shape of a perfect heart. What I saw blew me away! I was astonished and my spirit began to lift because I could feel God's love in what my eyes were beholding. Then, all of a sudden, the beautiful heart-shaped cloud began to open up and it was an angel with huge wings that unfolded, and then he flew away!

Immediately, my tears of sadness became tears of joy! I began praising God for the love He had shown me by sending an angel to visit me in a heart-shaped cloud just to say, "I love you." Angels are known as messengers from God, and I knew this was a message the Lord was sending me to let me know just how much He loved me.

The Bible tells us, "In everything give thanks; for this is God's will for you in Christ Jesus" (1 Thessalonians 5:18 NASB). This means that, even when we are hurting, somehow, we must muscle up the strength, to tell the Lord thank you. Unfortunately, most people when they are hurting, turn to a man or a woman, drugs or alcohol and even pills to medicate their pain. However, none of these things will heal our broken heart. God alone is the only one who can love, comfort, heal and strengthen us like no else can.

The Lord has blessed me and opened my eyes to see into the spiritual realm, and I began to see angels everywhere. The sky is filled with angels who are flying to and fro. Their wings are constantly in motion. Sometimes, I wonder if they are on an assignment, waiting for God to give them instructions to bring us, so that He can bless us. The Word of God declares, "Angels are only servants—spirits sent to care for people who will inherit salvation" (Hebrews 1:14 NLT). And I knew this visitation from an angel confirmed God's word is true.

The Bible also describes another angelic encounter. God sent an angel to Peter to lead him and even protect him from his enemies, and I believe God is still using angels to guide us on our personal journeys through life today.

> Suddenly an angel of the Lord appeared and a light shone in the cell. He struck Peter on the side and woke him up. "Quick, get up!" he said, and the chains fell off Peter's wrists. Then the angel said to him, "Put on your clothes and sandals." And Peter did so. "Wrap your cloak around you and follow me," the angel told him. Peter followed him out of the prison, but he had no idea

that what the angel was doing was really happening;
he thought he was seeing a vision. They passed the first
and second guards and came to the iron gate leading
to the city. It opened for them by itself, and they went
through it. When they had walked the length of one
street, suddenly the angel left him. (Acts 12:7–10 NIV)

This is a beautiful encounter of the powerful manifestation of God using an angel to provide instructions, protection, and deliverance. God is capable of doing anything, but the question is, do you believe He is able?

Jesus promised before He left this earth that He would not leave us alone and He would send the Holy Spirit to help us, comfort us, and teach us. The Holy Spirit will lead us and guide us to know and understand the truth. He will even show us things that are to take place in our future.

"When the Spirit of truth comes, He will guide you into all truth.
He will not speak on His own but will tell you what He has
heard. He will tell you about the future" (John 16:13 NLT).

When we spend quality time worshiping the Lord, we invite His presence into our lives. This is another way God touches us. As I mentioned before, I feel His touch the most when I am praising and worshiping Him. As I begin to worship, His love and presence is all around me as His Spirit fills the room. Others will feel His presence as well when they are in alignment with the Holy Spirit.

"God is a spirit: and they that worship Him must worship
Him in spirit and in truth" (John 4:24 KJV).

I truly believe our relationship with the Lord begins in heaven. He has been in a relationship with us all of our lives. That is why our relationship with God is spiritual. Life did not start at birth; it started in heaven before He sent us to the earth. Just listen to what the Lord told the Prophet Jeremiah in the Old Testament:

> *"I knew you before I formed you in your mother's womb.*
> *Before you were born I set you apart and appointed you*
> *as my prophet to the nations" (Jeremiah 1:5 NLT).*

In the New Testament Jesus said,

> *"For He chose us in Him before the creation of the world to be*
> *holy and blameless in His sight in love" (Ephesians 1:4 NIV).*

Have you ever wondered why babies aren't able to talk; yet they give the impression they see things. I believe it is because they have been in the presence of God in heaven, and they have seen so much in the spiritual world. However, they are unable to tell us what they have seen or heard. I believe if they were able to talk, they would tell us of about all the beautiful splendors and wonders of heaven.

A touch from God is also an encounter when His spirit and our spirit connect; therefore, it may not come in the form of an angel. Sometimes it's seeing a rainbow in the sky or feeling the warmth of the sun on your skin. Most importantly, always look with great expectation for a touch from God because He is there.

HE IS EVERYWHERE!

I received another touch from the Lord at the funeral of one of my former bosses. This was the first time I had ever attended a Catholic funeral. My plans were to pay my respects and leave shortly afterward. However, the Lord pressed in my spirit to go to the burial.

As the burial procedures were coming to an end, I noticed my boss's mom and she looked so lost and hurt and I wanted to go over and console her. At first, I was nervous because we were not acquainted with each other. Several people surrounded her, and I felt uncomfortable about approaching her.

Finally, I walked over and simply hugged her. To my surprise, she held onto me, and I held onto her. We never said one word, however, when the hug ended, she looked as if she had regained her strength. I saw the weight of her sorrow lift. Then, as I walked away from her and before I could get in my car, I broke down in tears. The grief I felt was so heavy; it was like nothing I had ever experienced before. I couldn't stop crying, and God spoke to me and said, that when she and I hugged, God allowed the mother's pain and sorrow to be transferred from her to me. It was totally supernatural!

After comforting my boss's mom and leaving the burial site, I was driving home and listening to CeCe Winans sing "How Great Thou Art." I looked into the sky and saw a vision of the Kingdom of Heaven. It was surrounded by gates and filled with castles, then miraculously, the pain and sorrow disappeared.

> *"Carry each other's burdens, and in this way you will*
> *fulfill the law of Christ" (Galatians 6:2 NIV).*

All we need is one touch from God. As an evangelical Christian pastor, Jessie Duplantis once said, *"A Close Encounter of the God Kind."* Because no one else is capable of doing for us what only Jesus can do.

The hour has come, and the time is now. God is moving and touching the hearts of those who really desire to know Him. All you have to do, is allow Him to put the broken pieces of your life back together again, with just one touch.

"And all the people were trying to touch Him, for power was coming from Him and healing them all" (Luke 6:19)

5

THE FIRST DANCE

$\mathcal{I}$t was a cool, sunny fall morning in 2003 and I vividly recall the Holy Spirit placing a strong desire in my heart to go for a walk at Shelby Farms. Shelby Farms is a beautiful park that sits on about 4,500 acres in the heart of Memphis, Tennessee. It is a very peaceful and serene environment filled with trees and lakes. At the time, I lived several miles away from Shelby Farms, but the distance did not matter.

I am not an early morning person and rising early was not something I enjoyed; neither am I accustomed to taking early morning walks. But this particular morning, the Spirit of God was beckoning me to come and spend time with Him, and I knew I had to go.

I grabbed my CD player and headphones and prepared for what would be a mind-blowing experience—a date with God. On my way to the destination, my mom called and asked if I could I pick up a relative who needed a ride home. I wanted to help, but I could not stand up the lover of my soul; He was waiting for me at Shelby Farms and I knew there was something He wanted to share with me.

I explained to my mom that I could not pick up my cousin because God was calling me, and I had to be obedient to the urging in my spirit. My mom has always been such a blessing in my life. She's my friend and a strong woman of God. Spiritually, she understood God was speaking to me; therefore, her response was: "Well, he will just have to wait."

My mom understood the importance of putting God first, and she supported me in doing so. It is good to have supportive people in your life that will help you and love you during your spiritual journey. However, there may come a time when the Lord may call us on an assignment, and our parents and other loved ones may not agree. But when you know it is God: it is always imperative to obey the Lord.

I arrived at Shelby Farms and put on my headphones and begin listening to, *Throne Room* by CeCe Winans. Worship music always ushers in the presence of God, and I'll never forget what happened next as the song titled, "Jesus, You're Beautiful," written by Nate Sabin begin to play. The music seemed to penetrate my soul as I walked around the lake and sang the melodies of the words unto the Lord.

All of a sudden, the water at the lake, which was brown, turned white as snow, and a misty cloud appeared on the water. What happened next utterly astonished me! I began to see angels of the Most High God emerge out of the clouds that hovered over the water. Some were playing musical instruments while they danced to the song as it was playing. Each angel did something different as they all ascended out of the mist. One by one, they gracefully danced to the song.

Seeing the angels was one of the most amazing sights I have ever seen. The angels were worshiping Jesus, but I could tell they were dancing for me as well. Totally in awe at this beautiful sight, I smiled as I watched the Angels' dance, which lasted for almost five minutes. They were graceful, and they moved to every beat and every word of the song, which said:

> Jesus, how can I tell You
> How beautiful You are to me
> Jesus, song that the angels sing
> Jesus, dearer to my heart than anything
> Sweeter than springtime

A DATE WITH GOD

Purer than sunshine
Ever my song will be
Jesus, You're beautiful to me.

As the song neared the end, the last angel watched me intensely. He knew I was watching him as well, in admiration and amazement. He danced gracefully to the closing lyrics of the song. As the final words came to an end, the last angel bowed gracefully to me and disappeared.

Immediately after the song ended, the lake returned to its natural color and the peace of God surrounded me. It surpassed all of my understanding. Even today, as I reflect back on that awesome day, my own mind is blown away when I think about the powerful manifestation of God's love He showed me that day. God loves us so much, and He is truly a wonder to behold. I am so convinced He wants to show you the miraculous too—when you only believe.

The heavenly vision I saw that morning of angels worshiping the Lord reminded me of the lyrics to a song written by *Hezekiah Walker:* "What a mighty God we serve. Angels bow before him. Heaven and earth adore Him! What a mighty God we serve." In the book of Revelation 5:11–12 we read:

> *Then, I looked and heard the voice of many angels, numbering thousands upon thousands, and ten thousand times ten thousand. They encircled the throne and the living creatures and the elders. In a loud voice, they were saying: "Worthy is the Lamb, who was slain, to receive power and wealth and wisdom and strength and honor and glory and praise!" (NIV)*

When we set aside time to worship God, our worship will usher in His presence. I believe we can all learn a lesson from the angels and the way they worship the Lord our God. They honor and respect Him for who He is. In heaven, angels praise the Lord day and night saying, "Holy, Holy, Holy is the Lord God Almighty, who was and is and is to come" (Revelation 4:8 ESV). That's worship!

God longs for us to have a relationship with Him because this is how we communicate and have fellowship with Him. It is a longing for Him that must come from the core of who we are. It is a desire to know and understand the love He has for us like never before. He wants us to search for Him with all of our hearts and go deeper in our quest to know Him, and the day we decide to search for Him with all of our hearts, we will find Him.

> *"But if from there you seek the Lord your God, you*
> *will find Him if you seek Him with all your heart and*
> *with all your soul" (Deuteronomy 4:29 NIV).*

Whether we admit it or not, we all know there is a God, because the creation of man, the earth, and the heavens declare His glory! Therefore, we owe Him our time, our praise and our adoration.

> *"For since the creation of the world God's invisible qualities—*
> *his eternal power and divine nature—have been clearly*
> *seen, being understood from what has been made, so that*
> *people are without excuse" (Romans 1:20 NIV).*

I am not sure where you are on your spiritual walk today. You may be lost, broken and searching for love in all the wrong places, but I want you to know that Love is also looking for you. We are sons and daughters chosen by God, and He wants to speak to the child in you that reflects the innocence you were born with before the world taught you to fear—the child who still believe dreams do come true. God is your King and He is pure, holy, and He would love to have this dance with you.

6

THE PROPOSAL

J graduated from the University of Memphis in May 2003, and I recall being so confused about my next steps in life. I thought obtaining a degree would give me fulfillment, but it was one of the most miserable times in my life. I still felt unfulfilled and unloved. I had a low-paying job, and I felt empty. I had accomplished my degree, but nothing had changed on the inside. It seemed as if the right doors just wouldn't open for me, and I knew God was trying to get my attention.

I was lost and tired and knew there had to be more to life than what I was experiencing. I wanted to move to Los Angeles to pursue a career in fashion design, but I couldn't save enough money; I felt stuck in Memphis. Nevertheless, God is so faithful in His love for us. He knew exactly how I was feeling, and He began to visit me. He appeared to me in visions, and each time He was fighting for my heart.

I began to feel a strong urge to restore my relationship with the Lord—my first love. He was pursuing me, and while I was looking for someone to fill the emptiness I had inside, what I didn't realize God's Spirit was already inside of me giving me everything I needed.

This was one of my lowest moments, and I found myself in a state of *rebellion, which* means going against God's will and His Word for our lives. I tried to find fulfillment in going to clubs, drinking and partying. I knew God was chasing me, but I wasn't ready to surrender. I recall being at my sister, Petra's house talking to my mom on the phone, and as I looked out of the window and I saw the face of a man in the trees.

I calmly told my mom, "I see the face of Jesus in a tree, and He is looking at me." My mom asked me how did He look, and I told her He looked sad. "He looks as if He's disappointed in me.' I could tell He longed for me, as His eyes pierced my soul, but I still was not ready to give up on the world and surrender my life to Him.

I felt like the rich ruler described in the Bible who wanted to inherit the Kingdom of God but didn't want to give up his worldly possessions. God's love and His amazing grace are so unfathomable. Although I struggled with surrendering to Him, He refused to give up on me, so finally, I accepted His invitation.

In His proposal, He asked me if I would allow Him to be Lord of my life— and not just part of my life, but Lord over every area! He wanted to be Lord over my relationships, which means He wanted me to pray and acknowledge Him before dating anyone. His desire is to lead us and order our steps in life, but in order for Him to do this we must allow Him to be Lord.

He wanted to be Lord of my finances, which means He wanted me to pray and ask Him how I should spend my money, where to invest, and ask Him who to bless. He wanted to be Lord over my career; therefore, He wanted me to pray and ask Him, "Lord lead me to the job you have for me and the people you want me to minister to." When we accept Jesus Christ as the Lord of our lives, the word *Lord* means master, ruler, or commander. *Lord* represents an authority figure, which is superior to all others. He is sovereign as our supreme ruler.

God is the CEO—the Chief Executive Officer—of the universe, and He wants to be Lord over every part of our lives, and not just on Sundays! He wants to give us a fresh start and be a part of our lives every day. He wants to cleanse us, heal us, and make us whole.

More importantly, the Lord was asking me to become His bride and to give Him my life as a living sacrifice, holy and acceptable to Him. This proposal is not only for me, but for all those who will accept Him as Lord.

> *"And so, dear brothers and sisters, I plead with you to give your bodies to God because of all he has done for you. Let them be a living and holy sacrifice—the kind He will find acceptable. This is truly the way to worship Him" (Romans 12:1 NLT).*

The Lord was inviting me to enter into a relationship with Him that would last forever! He wanted me to lose my life by serving Him and doing His will and then I would find my life, the life I had been searching for.

Many of us long to know our purpose in life—why we were created. We yearn to understand God's plan for us while we are here on earth. If this is you, then I encourage you to accept His proposal and allow yourself to become lost in Him because then and only then will you find your life and understand the reason why you were created.

> *"For whoever wants to save their life will lose it, but whoever loses their life for me will find it" (Matthew 16:25 NIV).*

~~~Obtaining favor from God.~~~

After I accepted the Lord's proposal, He began taking me into a new dimension in my life, and I knew the unmerited favor of God was upon me. He was teaching me how to live a life of holiness and how to trust and depend on Him. He spoke through the prophets in almost every church I attended and told me the angels walked with me. I had already had encounters with angels, but this time, I knew He was sending His ministering angels just as He had done for the men and women of God we read about in the bible.

God had spoken to me through many prophets and told me that, if I was obedient and finished this book, and worked with Him ministering to others, He would bless me. The Bible tells us: "Delight yourself in the Lord, He will give you the desires of your heart" (Psalm 37:4 ESV).

One night during a revival, I received a word of prophecy. God was sending me to Los Angeles to help actors and actresses, and they were waiting for my arrival. I accepted God's proposal and began preparing to move to Los Angeles on nothing but faith and a Word of prophesy from the Lord, and I believed Him.

I decided to say, yes to His proposal, and after I did, He revealed to me the things He had planned for my life. Not everything is revealed at once because I believe God wants us to trust Him every step of the way. Then, as we walk in obedience to His instructions, He will begin to unfold more and more of His plans to us.

Like our forefather, Abraham, who traveled to a land he knew nothing about, I sensed I was being called to do the same. I didn't know every detail of the plan, but my faith was anchored in the Lord and God was calling me on a journey that required separation from the familiar. I can recall everyone thinking I was crazy to take this leap of faith, however, I was married to God, and I believed He was able to do anything but fail.

One night I had a dream and, in the dream, I was sitting in a field of wheat. I was surrounded by who I believed to be great men of God: Abraham, Moses, Elijah and David. They were all teaching and ministering to me and I was trying to take in everything they were saying, because it was lot of information. I could tell they only had a short amount of time to speak to me. When I awoke from the dream, I knew that God was confirming He was indeed calling me to minister for Him and these were my teachers.

If you have never encountered a true prophet of the Lord or received a word of prophecy, I will tell you that prophecy is the testimony of Jesus Christ and a divine word or revelation from God giving us a glimpse of God's plan for our lives. When the prophet is real and God speaks through them, you can rest assured the words God speaks to you will come to pass.

> *"And it shall come to pass in the last days, saith God, I will*
> *pour out of my Spirit upon all flesh: and your sons and your*
> *daughters shall prophesy, and your young men shall see visions,*
> *and your old men shall dream dreams" (Acts 2:17, KJV).*

Let me stop and add this: God will back up everything He has spoken, and what I am about to share with you are real testimonies to the glory of God.

When I knew it was God's will for me to move to Los Angeles, I began searching for an apartment and showed my brother, Gavin the option I was considering. The rent was low and not in the best part of town. Then Gavin pointed to the apartment displayed on the front cover of the magazine which showed a new luxurious high-rise apartment in downtown Los Angeles and said, "Sister these are the apartments you need to move in." He said, "You're a princess and highly favored and God wants you to live in the best."

Therefore, by faith, I applied for the luxury high-rise apartment in downtown Los Angeles, although my job in Memphis only paid $9.00 an hour, but I had faith in what God had spoken. The rent was over $1,600 a month and required a $700 deposit. This was a huge act of faith, because I had recently been denied at two apartment complexes in Memphis.

After applying, I waited patiently to hear whether I had been approved. Then, one day I received a call from the leasing agent, and He was so excited to tell me, "You have been approved for the apartment!" The leasing agent was more excited than I was and said, *"You claimed it!"* He then told me I would be required to pay the first month's rent of $1,600 and a $700 deposit upon moving in. I had saved the first month's rent but didn't have the $700 deposit but a heart filled with faith.

By faith, I packed my bags and purchased a one-way ticket and headed to Los Angeles, because God had already prepared everything for me!

Did my income qualify me for the apartment? No, because $9.00 an hour wouldn't qualify me to live in a luxurious high-rise apartment, but the favor of God certainly did and I believed God and His Word, which declares:

> *"Now unto him, that is able to do exceeding abundantly above all that we ask or think, according to the power that worketh in us" (Ephesians 3:20 KJV).*

My family and friends knew I was moving to Los Angeles, but I never told anyone my rent was over $1,600 a month. Only my mother knew, but even she didn't know that I didn't have the deposit, but confidence in God.

My mother and brother were blessed to fly to Los Angeles to help me get moved in. When we arrived, I was somewhat hesitant about going to sign the lease because I didn't have the deposit. However,

A DATE WITH GOD

God spoke to me and told me to go because He had already opened a door for me.

When I arrived at the apartments, the leasing agent, Kristen took us on a tour. The apartments almost looked like a description of the Garden of Eden. It was filled with palm trees and the sidewalks through the apartments were paved with mosaic tiles and water fountains throughout the complex. The fitness center, meeting rooms, computer room were so state-of-the-art; and it was blowing my mind away to know the Lord was actually blessing me to move into something so beautiful. The swimming pool had cabanas, a Jacuzzi and private sauna, steam room and tanning bed, located on the second floor. The exercise room had glass windows where you could see inside the swimming pool. We also had a 24-hour security and concierge. We were in awe, as we looked at the beautiful artwork, portraits, the plush carpeting throughout the entire complex and the black grand piano that sit in the lobby because the apartments were absolutely breathtaking. Glory to God!

After the tour we returned to the office and Kristen asked me for the rent and the deposit. Feeling a little nervous, I gave her my rent, and then asked with confidence, if I could post-date a check for the deposit. Although doing this was against the property's policy, Kristen paused and said, "That will be fine."

We all felt a sigh of relief, because we knew the Lord had touched the heart of Kristen who extended the time for me to pay the deposit which lasted for almost a year. I will never forget the kindness Kristen showed me and my family.

The Lord had arranged everything so I moved into my new apartment with nothing but my clothes. My mom bought me an air mattress to sleep on and a few household things to get started. Having no furniture never bothered me, because I enjoyed coming home everyday spending quality time with Jesus. I never complained because I was just happy and content to be living out my destiny.

Eventually, I started to have pains in my back from sleeping on the air mattress; therefore, I purchased a wicker chair so I could at least have a place to rest my back. In spite of my circumstances, I still remained faithful in my walk with God and continued to share the Word of God on the movie sets and minister each time the Lord opened a door.

Just when sleeping on the air mattress began to feel unbearable, God sent Melanie a close friend to become my roommate. Her boyfriend at the time, who is now her husband purchased us a bed. Later, my friend Chasity came to visit me for Thanksgiving and purchased me a television.

Then the most amazing thing happened. I received a call from Brittney, one of my friends since college. Brittney called to say her aunt Debbie was getting married and asked if she knew anyone who needed furniture. Brittney told her about me. Although her aunt Debbie didn't know me, but God knew my circumstance and touched her heart to give me almost everything in her home. Glory to God!

When I arrived at her home, she greeted me so kindly and told me I could have everything and take whatever I needed. Brittney's aunt gave me a sofa and love seat, a bedroom suite, two televisions, two DVD players, pots and pans, dishes and she even offered me a piano, but my apartment was too small. I will always be grateful for the love and kindness Brittney's aunt showed me.

I praised and magnified the Lord like never before. I felt like I was living a Cinderella story, excluding the wicked godmother. I went to sleep with nothing and woke up with more than enough!!! Praise the Lord!!!

In one day, the Lord took me from an empty apartment with only an air mattress and a wicker chair, to an apartment filled with furniture! I am persuaded, because of all the Lord has done for me, when we take care of God's business, God will take care of our business.

When God speaks a Word concerning your future or a move He wants you to make, many times it is not wise to tell anyone until the prophecy has come to pass. Sometimes we can release information too fast, and the enemy will use even family, friends, or anyone to sow doubt, fear, and negativity in our minds. But you must remember, it is your faith that moves God; therefore, we must discipline ourselves to listen only to Him.

I recall arriving in Los Angeles and being so excited about the men and women who desperately needed a date with God. I knew God would use me to minister to them. God had spoken and said the actors and actresses needed me, so I began seeking Him for ideas to put His plan into action, and to find them because faith without works is dead.

I didn't have any acting experience, but one of my friends, Tia connected me with her uncle, Christopher Gray who is a casting director. He gave me my first acting gig as an extra, working with Tom Cruise in the movie *Collateral*. I knew it was the favor of God that had opened this door.

During my first week on the movie set, I begin sharing my faith with anyone who would listen. God is so amazing because acting has always been a desire of my heart. He will use you in the area of your gifting. While on the movie sets, the Lord blessed me to help so many people in such a short time. I ministered to everyone who desired to hear about the love and hope of Jesus Christ.

I recall one day on set seeing the late Isaac Hayes. Mr. Hayes was sitting near the director of the movie. When I laid eyes on him, I felt the urging of the Lord to go to him and introduce myself, since he was also from Memphis.

The other extras warned me I could not go near the director's area or where the movie stars' chairs were stationed. Being a daughter of the King, I did not listen to them. Therefore, I walked right up to Isaac Hayes and said, "Hi. My name is Alena Kelley, and I am from Memphis." Immediately, Isaac Hayes began laughing and talking to me as if we had known each other all of our lives.

Mr. Hayes asked me how long had I been in Los Angeles, and I replied a month. He was shocked that, after only one month, I had landed a spot as an extra on one of Tom Cruise's movies. However, I knew it was the favor of God that had positioned me to be on that set.

Mr. Hayes and I were laughing and talking like old friends when, to my surprise, Tom Cruise walked up and started talking to Isaac Hayes. I stood there in amazement because when others said it couldn't be done, I was now in the presence of both Tom Cruise and Isaac Hayes.

Isaac Hayes kindly introduced me to Tom Cruise as his good friend, Alena, from Memphis. We laughed and talked about one of Tom Cruise's movies filmed in Memphis called *The Firm*.

Tom Cruise jokingly said, "Alena, I did a whole lot of running in Memphis." (He was referring to his role in the movie.) I said, "You sure did." I shared with Tom Cruise my mom was offered a role as an extra in his movie, and Tom said, "Well, tell your mom I said hello."

Tom Cruise left me with a lasting impression because he was one of the kindest actors I have ever met. He introduced me to his personal assistant and told her, if I needed anything, he wanted her to take care of me. It was at that moment I realized God had me on a special assignment, and it all became real to me that night.

Although the scene I played in was cut, I knew my purpose was to take care of God's business and that is His people. He had opened a door for me to do exactly what He had said. The Bible tells us:

> "A man's gift makes room for him and brings him
> before great men" (Proverbs 18:16 KJV).

When we live a life that is pleasing to the Lord, we can expect the blessings and favor of God in our lives.

My mom later moved to Los Angeles and was employed by The Peninsula Beverly Hills where many high-profile guest and actors would often stay.

One day the actress Lynn Whitfield came to her office for assistance. Ms. Whitfield mentioned she was auditioning for a role in one of Tyler Perry's movies. Ms. Whitfield said she had faith and believed the Lord would bless her and stated she had received a prophecy and she shared it with my mother. Then, my mother told Ms. Whitfield her daughter had recently been anointed as a prophet and was blessed with the gift of prophecy as well.

Ms. Whitfield gave my mom her cell number and told her to have me call her because she wanted me to pray for her. My mom came home from work excited and told me, "Lynn Whitfield want you to pray for her." I became extremely nervous, because I had just became anointed by God as a prophet and was new in my calling.

I prayed for Ms. Whitfield as she had asked, and the Holy Spirit gave me a word of prophecy for her, although I never shared it with her. I knew Ms. Whitfield's request for prayer was another confirmation the Lord had sent me to Los Angeles to minister to actors and actresses. We later learned the Lord had blessed Ms. Whitfield and she received the exact role she had desired in Tyler Perry's movie.

I was blessed to share my faith with numerous people on different movie sets. I worked with several actors such as the comedian, Bernie Mac where I landed the role of a teenager. My character was a 15-year-old girl, and I was around 23 years old at the time. Bernie Mac saw the age difference and was calling me out. He walked over to me and asked, "Girl, how old are you? I know you not no teenager." I jokingly told him, "Gone, Bernie Mac" because I didn't want him revealing my age. Some of the other movies and TV shows the Lord blessed me to be a part of were *Fat Albert*, *Gilmore Girls, ER, Las Vegas, Woman Thou Art Loosed, Joan of Arcadia and Lackawanna Blues*.

During the filming of *Lackawanna Blues*, Terrance Howard encouraged the actors who were on set. Mr. Howard shared with us the blessing of being chosen to work on movie sets like *Lackawanna Blues*. Mr. Howard told us we should be happy to wake up every morning and be thankful for the opportunity to live out our dreams.

We must be confident in sharing our faith because others will sense when we are sincere and assured of the confidence we have in God. Each time I shared my faith with someone, I felt so fulfilled. When we minister to others the Word of God, we sow seeds into their heart.

The Bible tells us the Word of God is powerful, therefore; when we sow seeds by telling others how much Jesus loves them and the plans He has for their lives, we must be confident we have done our part in sharing our faith. However, after the seed has been planted, it must be watered. Watering takes place when God uses a pastor, a friend, or even a stranger to come along and pour God's Word into their lives again. Sometimes, we become disappointed when God allows us to speak into someone's life and we don't see an immediate change. But the Lord is the only one who can produce a harvest from our labor and because His Word is so powerful, you can have faith knowing that your labor will not be in vain.

"I have planted, Apollos watered; but God gave the increase" (1 Corinthians 3:6 KJV).

By now you are probably thinking, "Alena has had the best life ever, living in Los Angeles and acting with stars many of us only dream of meeting." However, my date with God has not always been picture perfect. God is perfect, but I was far from being perfect and had my own struggles when I became impatient and walked away from my date with God. As a result, I experienced my share of downfalls. The enemy tried to stop my destiny by sending the wrong people into my life but, God is so loving and He's able to restore.

In April 2005, while living in Los Angeles, I became pregnant and gave birth to my first son, Ayden Isaiah Kelley, whom I love with all of my heart. When I became pregnant with Ayden my career in acting was just taking off. I had just hired an agent and had appeared in the movie *Fat Albert*.

During my pregnancy, I became very ill and could no longer work, but the Lord blessed my mom and my brother to take over paying the rent, therefore, I knew the Lord used them to sustain me during that period of time.

One thing we must never forget, although the enemy may try to block our blessings, God still has a plan to bless us. The enemy will even present a proposal and use almost anyone to try to detour us from the plans God has for our life. However, make no mistake about it; his strategy will never stop the plans of God, as long as we walk in obedience to Him.

Little did I know Ayden would become one of my greatest blessings! Ayden gave my life so much meaning and he still does. Giving birth to Ayden caused me to become more determined and diligent in completing my mission for the Lord. Being a single parent is never easy and I understand the struggle, but I also know the blessing of having a child. Two years after giving birth to Ayden, I decided to relocate back home to Memphis because I wanted to raise my son around family and friends. However, in my heart I knew someday I would return to Los Angeles.

I never forgot the reason the Lord sent me to Los Angeles the first time, and I knew my mission had not been aborted. I was confident He would send me back again, but in His perfect timing not mine.

If you can relate to being a single parent, I want you to be encouraged, because God's proposal can never be canceled; neither can the enemy terminate the blessings God has for your life when we walk in obedience to Him. My mission was delayed, but it certainly was not denied.

"The Lord will call you back, as if you were a wife deserted and distressed in spirit—a wife who married young, only to be rejected," says your God. "For a brief moment I abandoned you, but with deep compassion, I will bring you back." (Isaiah 54: 6–7 NIV)

Evangelical pastor and author Rick Warren said, *"We are made for a mission."* We are shaped for ministry and serving God. Therefore, I encourage you to present yourself, your gifts and your talents to the Lord because He wants to use you for His glory.

When we accept the proposal from God to be His bride, we must be willing to become one with Christ, the same as we would become one with our mate in an earthly marriage. Your body now belongs to God, because He gave up His body and even His royalty just for you. Therefore, we must be willing to give up anything that tries to separate us from our relationship with the Lord, so that we can gain everything God has in store for us.

When someone proposes to you, everything changes. We move from being single to becoming engaged. Our minds begin to shift toward the day of being a bride or groom and becoming one: we adopt self-less love and a sacrificing mindset. Therefore, when the Lord asks for our hand in marriage, this is when the relationship with Him is restored and we begin to learn what true love really is. When we begin to truly comprehend God's love for us, we should have no problem being submissive to Him and obeying Him because He has our best interest at heart.

As with an earthly husband, our name changes, and so it is with the Lord as we become known as the bride of Christ. We are no longer independent, but with Christ as our husband and our King, we must allow Him to reign and rule over our lives because He loves us, and He knows what is best for us.

My prayer today is that you will decide to accept the Lord's proposal to become His bride. The Lord has promised when you say yes to Him, you will reap the benefits of His riches in glory and most importantly, eternal life. But don't be surprised when the world began to persecute you because of your faith. Just remember Jesus said, "Be of good cheer. I have overcome the world." God is on your side and He wants to see you reach your destiny.

He has a plan and purpose for your life and just as you would fight for your earthly marriage, you must continue to fight and let nothing separate you from the love God has for you.

> *"Who shall separate us from the Love of Christ? Shall tribulation, or distress, or persecution, or famine, or nakedness, or peril, or sword? As it is written, for thy sake we are killed all the day long; we are accounted as sheep for the slaughter. Nay, in all these things we are more than conquerors through Him that loved us. For I am persuaded, that neither death, nor life, nor angels, nor principalities, nor powers, nor things present, nor things to come, nor height, nor depth, nor any other creature, shall be able to separate us from the Love of God, which is in Christ Jesus our Lord" (Romans 8:35-39, KJV).*

No matter how tough the adversity, persecution, or battles you face throughout your relationship, God loves you and He knows the desires of your heart. If you will only say yes to the Lord's proposal and answer His call like me, you will see He has so many great plans prepared just for you.

7

THE MARRIAGE

*Y*ears ago, there was a casting call for the movie *One Night with the King*. The film was based on Esther, whom I mentioned earlier in chapter three. When I heard about the casting call, I became so excited. This was an opportunity of a lifetime. I auditioned for the part but was not selected. However, I was still excited just to be in the atmosphere of something great.

When the movie was released, it became one of my favorites. I love the story of Esther because God caused a Jewish woman to marry a Persian King, who was not a Jew, and had just divorced his wife, Queen Vashti, because she disobeyed the orders of the king. Therefore, Vashti was cast out from the kingdom, and God placed on the king's heart to choose Esther as his new queen.

After Esther was crowned queen, her uncle, Mordecai, learned of a plot to destroy all the Jews. Had this plot been carried out, it would have also included Esther since she was also a Jew, however, the King didn't know this when he married her. Therefore, Esther's uncle went to her in private and told her the scheme and pleaded with her to go to the king on behalf of the Jews and to save her own life.

During that time, no one could approach the king without approved permission; not even his wife. The penalty for anyone who dared to advance toward the king in this manner was inescapable death, except the king stretched out his royal scepter to the person approaching. Realizing the consequences could be deadly, Esther may have been apprehensive in approaching the king, however, Mordecai made a profound statement that not only proclaimed his faith in God, it also provoked Esther to consider why God had allowed her to become queen.

Listen to the words Mordecai spoke to Esther:

> *"If you keep quiet at a time like this, deliverance and relief for the Jews will arise from some other place, but you and your relatives will die. Who knows if perhaps you were made queen for just such a time as this?" (Esther 4:14 NLT).*

Now, let's hear Esther's profound response:

> *"Go, assemble all the Jews who are found in Susa, and fast for me; do not eat or drink for three days, night or day. I and my maidens also will fast in the same way. And thus I will go in to the king, which is not according to the law; and if I perish, I perish" (Esther 4:16 NASB).*

Esther understood the possibility of losing her life; however, her heart was filled with faith and determination, and she demonstrated her belief in God and honored His ability to grant her the respect and admiration of the king.

> *The king's heart is like channels of water in the hand of the LORD; He turns it wherever He wishes" (Proverbs 21:1).*

I am sure Esther was afraid, but the words of her uncle resonated in her spirit as she realized God had chosen her to be queen and placed her in the right place, at the right time, to save His chosen people from destruction. God used this anointed woman to expose the enemy and stop a conspiracy, that not only saved the Jews, but her own life as well. Then, God allowed the tables to be turned on their enemies to their own destruction.

A DATE WITH GOD

Isn't it amazing, how God ordained Esther to become the wife and queen to the Persian king, Ahasuerus, who had just divorced his former wife? But, God knew in order to save His people; Esther would need to be in position to carry out this awesome assignment.

"My thoughts are nothing like your thoughts,' says the Lord. 'And my ways are far beyond anything you could imagine. For just as the heavens are higher than the earth, so my ways are higher than your ways and my thoughts higher than your thoughts" (Isaiah 55:8–9 NLT).

As you can see, marriage is one of the most important and life-changing commitments one will ever make in life. God allowed Esther to marry King Ahasuerus because He needed someone who would be willing to sacrifice their very life, to save His people, and Esther was the woman for the job. While marriage may have its benefits for our personal lives, God also has an ordained purpose for marriage. Therefore, we should be sure the relationship we enter has been joined together by God.

The Lord's love for us runs deep and it's so beautiful that He even describes the church as His bride. Although earthly marriages are temporary, our marriage to Christ is forever. Remember, it is God who loved us first and He has gone above and beyond our expectations to prove His love for us. He is the only one who has demonstrated to us what true love really is.

"There is no greater love than to lay down one's life for one's friends" (John 15:13, NLT).

~~~~~~~~~~~~~~~~~~~

~~~*I was a little girl with a dream.*~~~

I was in the eighth grade in junior high and I recall telling God I desired to be married. Yes, I was way ahead of my time. As a child, I knew I wanted to be married and always desired to have a family. However, there was only one person who had my heart, and his name was Tony Harris.

I loved Tony before I understood what the word love truly meant. While I was in junior high, I prayed for him, wrote letters to God, and envisioned a life with him. I would look for him when I walked the halls at East High School in Memphis, Tennessee, and I would wait to get his attention.

I remember our first date, the summer of 1995: Tony picked me up from home, and we went to the movies. It was the quietest ride, and once we arrived, we were like two children, but he was so respectful the entire time. When the night came to an end, it was the most innocent date I had ever had. It was my first date, and he was a perfect gentleman.

After he kissed me goodnight, I went inside, closed the door, and dropped to the floor! I had always wanted to drop to floor like the girls on television. I was giddy as a little girl whose dream had finally come true. It was the best night of my life.

After our initial date, Tony and I didn't go on another date in high school. At the time, I didn't understand why, but I realize now that my timing did not correlate with the time God had appointed for us to connect. I saw Tony every day at school, and I believe we both felt the same chemistry for each other, but neither of us knew how to express what we were feeling. However, I knew in my heart one day it would all come together.

I'm sure I wasn't the only girl at school attracted to Tony, however, I believe the calling God had on my life is what separated me from the other the girls. I was not sexually active, and I was not aggressive with Tony. I never approached him or did anything unbecoming as a young woman of God. I kept what I felt for Tony in my heart because I trusted God with my secret desires.

Because I surrendered my life to the Lord at a young age, trusting God was instilled in me. My mom had raised us in a Christian home, and I understood the importance of having patience and waiting for the desires of my heart. However, during the waiting process we must stay prayerful, because our flesh will become impatient, and the enemy will tempt us to consider other options.

> *"Do not be anxious about anything, but in every situation,*
> *by prayer and petition, with thanksgiving, present*
> *your requests to God" (Philippians 4:6 NIV).*

Three years had passed and Tony and I still had not connected, then someone else began to pursue me and I entered another relationship. However, things really became complicated when Tony began to realize I was the one for him and we both felt the connection.

I recall one cold winter night attending a high school party and Tony was also there. Tony and I connected on a different level and this had never happened before. We laughed and played the whole night, and everything seemed perfect.

When it was time to go home, Tony's cousin, my beloved friend, the late Kena "Shea" Blakney, picked us up from the party to take us home. Tony and I lived in the same neighborhood, but the drive from the party to home felt like an eternity. Snow had fallen, and the streets were covered with ice, therefore, Shea was very careful and drove extremely slow. I knew she was giving us as much time as possible to spend together.

Shea was one of my closest friends and she's also Tony's cousin, but I called her my sister. Shea always believed Tony and I were destined to be together. When I think about it, I believe it was the Lord using Shea because she tried so hard to connect us. She did everything humanly possible trying to make it happen. I recall on one occasion, Shea even cried when she saw Tony and I were drifting apart.

As Shea drove us home that night from the party, I remember the song *"Every time I Close My Eyes,"* written and performed by *Babyface*, came on the radio. The words of the song resonated with both our spirits, and we both felt the lyrics go through us, connecting our hearts. Shea felt it too. Usually she's very talkative, but that night she was quiet as a mouse. Shea knew something special was happening. These are the words to the song:

> Girl, it's been a long, long time comin'
> But I, I know that it's been worth the wait
> It feels like springtime in winter
> It feels like Christmas in June
> It feels like heaven has opened up its gates for me and you
> And every time I close my eyes
> I thank the Lord that I've got you

As the song played, I knew in my heart and in my spirit Tony was still the one. Although I was dating someone else, everything in that moment confirmed, I was destined to be with Tony. Nothing and no one else mattered that night. It felt like the lyrics of the song literally came to life and heaven had opened its gates for me and Tony.

Shea dropped me off first, and then she drove Tony home. About twenty minutes later, I received a phone call from Shea and she was so excited and said, "Girl, you ain't gone believe this! Lena, Tony wants to be with you!"

I had been waiting since the eighth grade to hear those words, however, impatience had gotten the best of me, and I had already committed myself to another relationship. Sadly, I felt bound to stay in a relationship that was not God's destiny for me. I believe in being faithful and thought I couldn't say yes to Tony, even though, deep in my heart, I wanted to be with him. If only I had been patient and waited.

Tony was the man of my dreams, and my commitment to the wrong person was a huge mistake, because eventually he betrayed me, and I was heartbroken. This was a painful lesson for me, therefore, I would admonish you to consider, the enemy could possibly send the counterfeit before the promise arrives.

Tony watched as I went through this difficult time and was there for me as a friend. I could see in his eyes, he wished he could take away all the hurt.

Tony was a McDonald's All-American and the number-one-point guard in the country. As he prepared to leave for college, Tony came to me and offered me a full scholarship to attend University of Tennessee Knoxville with him, but I didn't accept it and to this day I'm not sure why I turned his offer down.

Not choosing Tony back then was a decision I still regret to this day. I regret wasting so much time in the wrong relationship and if only I had said yes to Tony in 1997, it might have saved both of us from so much heartache and disappointment.

Tony and I had gone our separate ways to college, then finally during his senior year we began dating again. I was so in love. I remember having some fun times with Tony during college. At times our relationship was perfect; however, there were other times when I saw he had trust issues. I didn't understand at the time how much he was battling to have genuine people in his life.

It wasn't long before the relationship between me and Tony began to fall apart again, because I was looking for Tony to fill a place in my heart that only God can fill. I was no longer the little girl with a dream of her knight in shining armor coming to her rescue. Life had somehow managed to scar me, and Tony was also broken because so many people had used him and taken advantage of his ability to play basketball. As an athlete who had a promising future in the NBA, Tony didn't know who he could trust.

Therefore, Tony needed friends and family who genuinely loved him and had no hidden agendas. We both felt as if we had been robbed of our dreams for the future, which left both of us broken and in need of a healer.

I knew God was trying to get my attention because He wanted me to commit my life to Him. As a result of my decision, I had to separate from friends, because our lives were on two different paths, but I had made a promise to God—a commitment to serve Him and do a work for Him—and I wanted to keep my word.

One day after getting off the phone with Tony, I heard something in his voice that didn't sound right. He sounded as if he didn't want to be bothered. I felt his pain, but I didn't know how to reach him. As the conversation ended, tears began to fall from my eyes, and I told the Lord repeatedly, "I trust You, God. I trust You, God."

That same evening, I decided I would go to church because being in the presence of God always made me feel better and helped me forget about my pain. This is one of the ways we cast our cares on the Lord.

This occurred on Wednesday, April 24, 2002. I was so hurt because things were not the same between Tony and me. It felt as if a wall was being built between us, and it broke my heart. I continued to cry out to the Lord as I drove to church. I kept telling God, no matter what happened, I still trusted Him. Even though I wanted to be with Tony more than anything else in the world, I knew God wanted me to be with Him more than anything as well.

As I drove down the 240 West Expressway in Memphis, I looked up at the sky and saw the most beautiful rays of light beaming from heaven. Amazed by the beautiful sight, in the midst of my pain, I began to thank the Lord as I tried to drive and watch the sky at the same time. As I glanced up at the sky again, I saw a cloud in a very unique shape, but I couldn't determine what it was.

As I continued to watch the sky, I noticed that the cloud had transformed into an angel with huge wings. I blinked my eyes several times because I wanted to make sure I wasn't seeing things. But after blinking, I realized the angel was still there. I watched the angel for a few minutes, and as he began moving closer to my car, I became nervous, but I was not afraid. I just wanted to make sure I was not losing my mind.

As the angel approached, I eased my hand down to the middle compartment of my car to get my cell phone, hoping the angel wouldn't see me. I wanted to call my mom and tell her what I was witnessing. I could tell he knew exactly what I was doing, and he disappeared. My drive to church was filled with so many questions:

Why had the angel appeared? Why was the angel sent to me? Was he coming to bring me a message, and would I see him again?

When I arrived at church, I shared with my mom what I had experienced, and she was so excited. She knew the hand of God was on my life and was not surprised about my visitation of an angel, but instead she rejoiced.

After the visitation from the angel that day, Tony and I would not reconnect in a relationship for twelve long years. I endured twelve years of being hurt by men who claimed they loved me, but the reality was that they never did. It took me twelve years of being disappointed, until I finally realized God was lovingly allowing me to be broken so that He could make me over again.

This wasn't the first encounter my mom believed I had experienced with an angel. She shared with me an encounter I had with a little girl when we lived in Binghampton, and I was only around five or six years old. My mom saw me playing one day with a little girl she had never seen before in our neighborhood. That same day she had read in her Bible the passage where Jesus said, if you give a drink of water to one of His little ones, you have done it unto Him.

After playing for a while, me and the little girl became thirsty and she came into the house with me and asked my mom for a drink of water. My mom asked me who was the little girl and if I knew where she lived. I told her she was my friend, and we had been playing together. My mom told her she should be careful going into people homes she didn't know and asking for water.

The little girl quickly ran out the house, and immediately my mom knew God was allowing the scripture to be fulfilled. She ran outside trying to catch the little girl to offer her some water, but she had disappeared. When my mom could not find her, she was heartbroken because she knew we had just entertained an angel. We never saw the little girl again.

> *"Do not forget to show hospitality to strangers, for by so doing some people have shown hospitality to angels without knowing it" (Hebrews 13:2 NIV).*

In 2013, I traveled to Las Vegas to attend the Magic Show. While on Instagram, I saw a post on Meagan Good's page for a casting call featuring her husband, Devon Franklin who was a guest on Oprah Winfrey's new televised show on OWN called *The Help Desk*. Impressed by the Lord to go and audition, I drove from Las Vegas to Los Angeles where the casting call took place. When I arrived on the set, there was a line of people who had also come to audition. While standing in the line, I overheard staff members telling people who were ahead of me that they were not accepting any more actors.

I walked up to the front of the line, and the producer asked me for my name. I told her my name was Alena Kelley and that my name was not on the list. She stared at me for a minute and then said, "Come with me." She sat me down with the other cast members. I knew it was the favor of God upon my life that had caused this to happen.

I was interviewed for the part, then after the audition, I was blessed with the opportunity to speak with Devon Franklin one on one. I told him of my desire to move back to Los Angeles. Devon told me, "After you complete God's assignment for you in Dallas, you should move to Los Angeles." I told him I was a single parent and he told me being a single parent in Hollywood would be hard and he advised me to not come alone. Basically, he was indicating I should wait on God.

After my trip to Vegas, I returned to Dallas with a new mindset and was motivated by my experience with Devon Franklin. A year had passed and I was at work when I received a call from a classmate, who also lives in Memphis. She called to tell me that Tony had become a minister. I was so excited to hear he had surrendered his life to the Lord. I shared the news with my mom and coworkers. I told my mom that Tony was walking in his calling, and she should be walking in her calling as well. After hearing the news about Tony, we both knew we should be doing the work God had called us to do. I knew if Tony was walking in his calling, there was no excuse for us to not walk in ours.

Within thirty minutes after hearing the news that Tony had become a minister, I received a text message from Tony that said: "Hey, Lena, this is Tony. I just wanted to let you know I am a minister now." He included an image of his license showing that he had been ordained. I was totally blown away and couldn't believe all this was happening consecutively. Because only God could allow such timing: I was discussing Tony with my coworker, Patricia in Dallas, TX and within 30 minutes I received a text message from Tony who was in Memphis, TN. I couldn't believe all this was occurring, as I received a text message from my first love, Tony Harris. God had allowed him to find me and it was so amazing how it all happened. Tony had tracked my number down from someone, and when I received the text from him, I was totally blown away!

When Tony and I spoke by phone, he told me God had called him to be a minister, and he was preaching the gospel. He said the Lord had stopped him while he was in the middle of cleaning and prompted him to call me. Tony told me, at first, he thought, "Okay, I will call her later." But as he continued to clean, the Holy Spirit spoke to him again and said, "Call Alena now!"

He said God spoke with such urgency, he felt if he did not call right then, he was going to be in trouble with the Lord. When he called, I was so glad to hear from him, and so proud of his new life in Christ. We immediately began a friendship centered on the Lord. There were no old feelings from the past. We were just two friends who had found Christ and were so excited to share with each other all we had learned. This time, our friendship was built on a solid rock: Jesus Christ!

Shortly into our friendship, I received a phone call from my spiritual mother, Prophet Delisha Rushing who I call momma Delisha. She said God had dropped me in her spirit and she asked me if her fiancé at that time, Prophet Zebelum K. Rushing, could pray for me. I had never met him, but I trusted he must be a man of God if she wanted him to pray for me. Momma Delisha would always encourage me to wait on the Lord because He had blessed her with a man who loved the Lord and loved her too. She was certain that, if the Lord had blessed her, He would do the same for me or even greater. It always amazed me when she said, "God will do the same for you or greater when you wait on God."

As I spoke with Prophet Rushing he began to pray and the Spirit of God began to fill my car. The presence of God was so powerful, I had to pull over, and it was not a coincidence that I pulled onto a church parking lot.

As the Lord began to speak through Prophet Rushing, he began to prophesy and told me, "You bank with Regions." To my astonishment, this was my bank and I replied, "Yes, I do." I actually had two bank accounts, but Regions was the only bank I was doing business with at the time. Then, Prophet Rushing said my mother had prayed the prayer of faith, and God would not let any harm come to me.

The Lord then told Prophet Rushing to tell me to be careful of a man who was in my past and be watchful and prayerful. He also prophesied that I would own my own fashion business, and God would give me favor with women who would appreciate my walk with the Lord and this would open doors to my destiny. The Lord said this was the life He had for me, and everything he said was exactly what I had envisioned since I was a little girl. The Lord said I was not just any woman, I was a queen and I deserved to be treated like one.

Then Prophet Rushing said the Lord told him I had the attention of an athlete who was watching me. At this point, my spiritual mom asked me if I knew any athletes, and I said no! She asked me again if I was sure, and God spoke to me and said, "Tony." So, I called Tony's name out loud.

Prophet Rushing then said, "Tony Harris." At this point, I was really blown away and didn't know what was happening. He then told me everything God spoke to him about Tony. I had not given him Tony's last name, so I knew God was speaking through him. The man of God also didn't know, from the first time I saw Tony in the eighth grade, I had known he was my husband, but I kept that belief in my heart.

Prophet Rushing prophesied how my marriage would be totally different and concluded by telling me that Tony Harris was my husband and God had ordained him for me from the foundation of the world. He said I would be moving to Los Angeles, and Tony would support me. The Lord also said we would start off in a studio apartment in Glendale, California. I didn't understand why the Lord would send us to Glendale because, having lived in Los Angeles, I had no knowledge of Glendale, but I believed the Lord's instructions.

So many people desire to hear a word of prophecy from the Lord, but we must be careful because the Bible tells us many false prophets have gone out into the world, deceiving many. After Jesus was crucified and ascended back into heaven, He sent His Holy Spirt who has given gifts to the body of Christ to edify us which means to instruct or improve someone morally or intellectually and build us up, but we must study the Word of God to understand the difference between what is real and what is counterfeit, otherwise we can easily be deceived by false prophets.

There are two Greek words that describe the scriptures: First Logos refers to the written Word and Rhema which refers to the utterance or spoken Word of God. For clarification Prophet Rushing explained it this way:

"This is how you will know the difference when what is spoken comes from the gifts of the Holy Spirit. The Spirit of Jesus Christ is the Spirit of prophecy and the gifts of His Spirit are broken down into three parts: revelation gifts, vocal gifts and power gifts. Whenever someone is used under the prophetic anointing of God, it will always line up with the Word of God, which is known as the Logos.

Whenever God gives a Rhema Word is it always given from the Logos the written Word of God. According to John 1:1- In the beginning was the Word and the Word was with God and the Word was God. Before we can get a revelation through Rhema there must be a revelation of the Logos.

The written Word is living revelation and the revelation gifts are:

- The word of knowledge
- The word of wisdom
- The discerning of spirits

Next you have the vocal gifts which we speak out of our mouths:

- The interpretation of tongues
- Divers kinds of tongues
- The gift of prophecy

Next you have the power gifts:

- Gifts of faith
- Gifts of healing
- Working of miracles

When the prophetic comes forth and God inspires the prophet to speak the oracles of God from the mouth of God, the prophet is going to flow in those revelation gifts, vocal gifts and power gifts. This is how we know it is inspired by the Holy Ghost. For the witness of the Holy Ghost is to bear witness of the Word of God and His job is to bear witness of Jesus Christ who the bible says is Emmanuel, God with us.

In the Book of 1 Cor. 12:8-11 - We must understand the Holy Spirit not only operate through the gifts of the Spirit, but also through the fruits of the Spirit. Gal. 5:22: The fruits are love, joy, peace, forbearance, kindness, goodness, faithfulness, gentleness and self-control" and against these there is no law. These are manifestations of love and they operate in the life of the believer.

Ephesians 4:11-12 speaks about the fivefold ministries and the governmental ministries. In the fivefold you have the apostle, prophet, evangelist, pastor and teacher. It is necessary to have the fivefold operative in the local church, to edify the church and to help us mature in the faith and to be balanced in the word of God. We must be strategic in the Word of God and be apt to learn and teach sound doctrine. Anyone who is not operating in the gifts of

God and the fruits of the Holy Spirit are not operating by the power of God."

~~~~~~~~~~~~~~~~~~~~~~

After I received the word of prophecy from Prophet Rushing, so many thoughts were going through my head about Tony and I needed confirmation. Therefore, I asked my son, Ayden, who was eight years old at the time, what was his opinion about Tony. I showed him a picture of Tony on Facebook. My son didn't know Tony personally, but God has often used Ayden to confirm things with me, and I trusted what he would have to say.

Ayden looked at Tony's picture and said, "Mom, he is a good man. He is a sweet man and a kind man. He is nice to the ladies and gentlemen, and he is a pastor!" My mouth flew open because I could not believe what I was hearing! Was this my confirmation?

I called my mom and told her, and she said, "Lena, I already knew Tony was your husband." So, this became a little frustrating to me. Why would God drop this information on me like this? Why did He not tell Tony first?

What was I going to do with this information? I certainly was not going to tell Tony! My mom told me to go home and pray. She said, "God speaks to you, so go into your prayer closet."

I prayed and asked the Lord if this was truly His will. I cried and prayed for days and did not hear anything. Then, one day it happened while I was at the dentist's office. I heard God call my name. He told me that Tony was my husband, and He said Tony was a man after His own heart. He said that Tony would love me because he also loved Him. Then, the Lord said that my heart and

Tony's heart were one. I was amazed that God had answered my prayer and given me the confirmation: Tony is your husband.

After receiving this confirmation from the Lord, I made the decision that I was not going to tell him. Tony and I spoke to each other almost every day and I had known this for almost three to four months, but never said a word. Keeping this to myself was extremely hard because I wanted to let Tony know, but I also wanted him to choose me on his own. I did not want him to feel forced.

I can remember times when we were talking, both of us would say the same thing at the same time, or Tony would know when something was going on with me because the Lord would tell him. Tony is a giver, and he was always giving or helping me in some way. He would give his time, his resources—whatever he had. There was not anything I lacked during our friendship. Even now he is an excellent husband, father and provider and I had never been treated this way before.

My loving Father explained to me why the other relationships had not worked. We typically pray for what we want instead of praying, "Lord, let thy will be done." God explained to me how so many of His children have missed His perfect will and the blessings He has for them. We plan our own lives and try to make relationships work that are not ordained by God. To do this is disobedience and when we act in disobedience to the plan God has for our lives, we can easily miss the very thing we desire.

God later told me, because I had finally put Him first, and kept my promise to give myself to Him, He was now giving me my soul mate. The husband He had ordained for me to marry before the foundation of the world.

A DATE WITH GOD

Shortly after I received the prophecy regarding Tony, the Lord spoke to Tony and told him I was his wife. In obedience to God and in his love for me, Tony asked me to marry him ... and my answer was *yes!* The Word of God tell us:

> *"He who finds a wife finds what is good and receives*
> *favor from the Lord" (Proverbs 18:22 NIV).*

February 15, 2015 the Lord blessed Tony and I to finally become husband and wife. It took Tony several years, but he finally found me. We both went through twelve years of highs and lows, disappointments, let downs, heartbreaks, rejection, and abandonment. We both had been on our own personal journeys of hurt and pain, but finally, when Tony submitted his life to the Lord and answered the call on his life to become a minister, God opened doors that freed both of us from captivity and the enemy no longer had us in bondage.

God created man to be the head and holds him accountable for his family. When the man becomes fully obedient to God's voice and instructions, his destiny is unlocked and he enters the perfect will of God. By submitting himself to walk in obedience to the Lord, He is positioning himself to receive everything rightfully his through Jesus Christ.

Also, when the man is walking in obedience to God the woman is also released from bondage, and God can connect the two to become one; the marriage God has ordained since the beginning of time. This was the case with Tony and myself. When Tony answered God's call, and I also surrendered my life to the Lord, we were both released from the former relationships that were never God's plan.

Tony shared with me how the Lord kept waking him up at 12:04 a.m., telling him he would preach His gospel and save many souls for Him. This was Tony's date with God, and when he accepted God's invitation, the Lord answered the prayer made by a twelve-year-old girl, twenty-three years ago.

God, in His sovereign power and love for His children, has already predestined and ordained a plan for each one of our lives. But it is our responsibility to seek to have the relationship with God that He is so desperately longing for. I believe when we do this and practice keeping God first, the mate He has for us will know it in his or her heart. When that mate does come along, our spirit will bear witness with their spirit that he or she is the one. We will know the truth, and the truth will set us free.

In 2016, I finally became obedient and completed what God had asked me to do, and that was to finish this book. The Lord wanted me to go into ministry and work with Him to reach lost souls who were hurting.

But the story does not end here. In December 2016, we received a supernatural visitation from God. I was nine months pregnant with our first son, Tony Jr. and living in God's promise daily. This pregnancy was very special to me because I had suffered a miscarriage the year before, but God spoke through Prophet Rushing and said there was an embryo behind the embryo and it was God's will that I have a child with my husband. God also spoke through Prophet Rushing and told me my faith would pay off and that I would be like Hannah in the bible and that I would conceive a child.

One day Tony and I came home after running errands. Tony went upstairs. I sat at the kitchen table and noticed the face of a man on the wall. It was the same face I had seen in the tree almost twenty years ago, but this time he wasn't sad. This time His face was radiant and full of glory!

When I saw the face of the Lord it surprised me and I screamed, "Baby, there is a man on the wall!" Tony answered, "Huh?" I screamed again, "There is a man on the wall!" Tony came downstairs, and we both knew it was Jesus. His face was radiant, bright and powerful.

Prophet Rushing told us later that it had been Jesus peeping in on us from heaven. The Lord's appearance was a confirmation to the prophecy we received from Prophet Rushing in September 2016 that God was going do something that was mind boggling and supernatural. We truly thank God for allowing a true prophet of God to be our spiritual father.

We considered this supernatural visitation to also be a date with God, but this time it was one I could share and experience with my entire family. The face of Jesus appeared on our wall almost every day at around 2:00 in the afternoon. Some days His face shifted from one side of the wall to the other side. As Tony and I praised and worshiped Him, His face begins to glow and radiate like the sun. Sometimes his appearance grew in stature.

On December 22, one day before Tony, Jr., was born, Jesus appeared again, and we believed in our spirit that He appeared to let us know that all was well. Tony Jr. was born the next day, December 23, 2016, however, he came into the world barely breathing, and his complexion was blue. The nurses immediately begin to clear his passage so that he could breathe. After I came from recovery little Tony's breathing still was not right. My husband noticed it first and we brought it to the nurse attention and she waived it off, saying he just needed to adjust to his new environment.

When I Facetimed my cousin, Charo she said, "Lena his breathing is not right. Have the doctor check him out?" We then requested another check-up and they discovered our son had too much fluid in his lungs and the hospital decided to keep him in ICU and said he wouldn't be able to go home with us on December 26th. But I remembered the word of God spoken through Prophet Rushing that all is well with the baby. He told me months before our son was delivered that you and the baby will leave the hospital together.

My husband and I begin to speak God's word and remind Him of His promise to us. And even though the doctor was saying one thing, we believed the report of the Lord. On December 26th our baby was released to go home with us, just as the Lord had spoken through Prophet Rushing.

Since the first time the face of Jesus appeared on our wall, we have received several visitations from Him. We believe Jesus is making his appearance for several reasons, but one special reason was to save our baby boy! Glory to God!!! I praise Him because He's an awesome God and watches over His children.

After our son was born, God showed us the power of a date with God. He explained the significance of a date with Him. Once we returned home with the baby, Jesus was waiting for us because He had now come to have a date with our son.

We knelt before Jesus and lifted the baby up before Him and spoke God's blessing over his life. My older son, Ayden, was able to experience a date with God as well with us on that day.

Soon after Jesus appeared on our wall, I searched Google for others who had seen Jesus through a vision or visitation. Then, I remembered Colton Burpo, the boy whose story is told by Todd Burpo and Lynn Vincent in their book, *Heaven is for Real: A Little*

Boy's Astounding Story of His Trip to Heaven and Back. I realized his image shown of Jesus is a very close representation of the Savior whom I witnessed during His visitation in my home.

After the encounter in our home, the face of Jesus disappeared, and we didn't have another visitation for almost a year. We thought the encounter was over but to our surprise I received a text message on November 27, 2017 from my husband saying Jesus was back. He showed up on the wall again around the same time He did last year, which was right before Christmas and He has been appearing almost every day. This now makes two years in a row that we have been experiencing our amazing date with God

We were blessed with the opportunity to capture pictures and videos of His appearance. God spoke to my heart to release one of the photos in this book. The other pictures and videos will be released by the leading of the Holy Spirit.

Our family will never forget how special a date with God is and He has truly touched our lives, and we know we have been chosen to work with Him to bring others into the Kingdom of God.

I wanted to share my experiences and my love for Christ with the world. The anointing God has placed on our lives is not only for us, but for all who will only believe. It was prophesied years ago that, through my ministry of fashion and building God a house of fashion, the clothes I designed or touched would carry an anointing so powerful that people would find deliverance through wearing these holy garments.

In the summer of 2017, Prophet Rushing told my husband and I, that God wanted us to start a church in Los Angeles. My husband and I obeyed and on January 7, 2018, Oasis West Church of Los Angeles was birthed here in Glendale, California under the leadership of my husband with Prophet Zebelum K. Rushing as our spiritual covering. We know this is our assignment from God and what a beautiful script He has written for all of us to share in His glory.

You see our life here on earth is a journey. It is like a book that has already been written. You only need to walk with God and ask for understanding when you reach a new chapter in your life. Just keep asking Him to lead you on the journey He has for you because, after all, it is His story.

God is the author and finisher of our faith. In other words, God is the writer, the Creator, of this entity called life. He alone is the reason we have started our journey with Him, and He alone will teach us how to finish it.

> *Being confident of this very thing, that he which hath begun a good work in you will perform it until the day of Jesus Christ" (Philippians 4:6, KJV).*

Life will have many challenges, and your faith will be tried, but I encourage you to keep walking with God through every chapter of your life. And, if you are dedicated to finish the book of life God has written for you, I guarantee you—you will reach your happily ever after.

But remember—it all starts with a *Date with God.*

Supernatural Visitation with Jesus

*The LORD make His face shine on you, and be
gracious to you; The Lord lift up His countenance to
you, And give you peace. Numbers 6:25-26*

CPSIA information can be obtained
at www.ICGtesting.com
Printed in the USA
BVHW030037021221
622945BV00001B/11

9 781973 619260